CONTENTS

GOOD SPELLING

Fun with English

w s

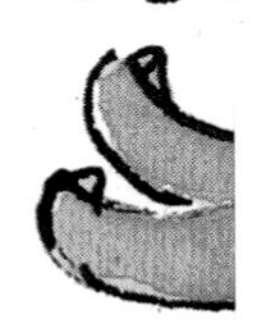

The author wishes to express his particular gratitude to Robert Wheeler, the designer of this book. There has been an especially close collaboration at every stage and the author has found this an immense stimulus and encouragement. The author would also like to thank Dr Trevor Pateman and Karen Wilbraham, who collaborated with him in the planning of this book, and Terry McKenna for his superbly amusing illustrations.

KINGFISHER
Kingfisher Publications Plc
New Penderel House
283-288 High Holborn
London WC1V 7HZ

First published in hardback
by Kingfisher Publications Plc in 1998
ISBN 0 7534 0300 5
2 4 6 8 10 9 7 5 3 1

First published in paperback
by Kingfisher Publications Plc in 1998
ISBN 0 7534 0280 7
2 4 6 8 10 9 7 5 3 1
BST/0600/WKT/--/128KTMA

Material in this edition was previously published in 1995
by Chambers in four separate volumes: *Fun with English: Good Spelling, Good Words, Good Grammar* and *Good Writing.*

A CIP CATALOGUE RECORD FOR THIS BOOK
IS AVAILABLE FROM THE BRITISH LIBRARY

Editor: John Grisewood
Illustrations: Terry McKenna
Design: Robert Wheeler Design Associates
Phototypeset by Southern Positives and Negatives (SPAN), Lingfield, Surrey
Printed in Hong Kong/China

Ingredients

Spelling

Spellings come from spells. As any good dictionary will tell us, there are three kinds of spells.

* There is what we do when we write.
* There is a spell of time.
* And there is magic.

We learn spelling by taking time to discover the magic of writing words.

We begin here with the magic – take a look at these 26 little squiggles.

We turn them around and – *Hey Presto!* – we have all the letters of the alphabet.

abcdefghijklmnopqrstuvwxyz

We mix them all around, lots and lots of them. And – *Hey Presto* – we can make thousands upon thousands of different words:

> **kind** words – **bad** words – **sad** words – **happy** words – **funny** words – **fine** words – **easy** words – **hard** words
> **adjectives – nouns – verbs – adverbs – pronouns**
> **homophones – homonyms – palindromes – onomatopoeia**

There are so many words that no one person can possibly count them all, know them all or even spell them all.

But there is magic about them: the magic that helps everyone know so many of them so quickly, so that we hardly realize what is happening.

Spelling is a **funny business**.

Some people **love** it, some **people don't.**
Sometimes it **comes**, sometimes it **won't.**
Sometimes it is **fun**, or it is just **work** to be done

but sometimes . . .

it is simply 

Some people are lucky. They pick up spelling without trying very hard at all.

Most of us have a bit of trouble in learning to spell. We have to work hard at it and put up with making lots of mistakes. But we usually learn to spell all right in the end.

Just a few of us have a terrible time with spelling. We have to work extra hard at it and then we still don't always get it right, even though we might be brilliant at other things such as reading, swimming or drawing.

In this book we want to give everybody another chance. We introduce a dozen different ways of learning how to spell. Readers can try each one and then see which ways suit them best. It is not a book to test you. It is a book for you to test.

But be careful! This book is dangerous. Keep it safe!

Words will stare you in the face. Your ears will deceive you. Rules will be broken. Spelling has magic power. No one can argue with good spelling.

Spelling is a very funny business. You are warned!

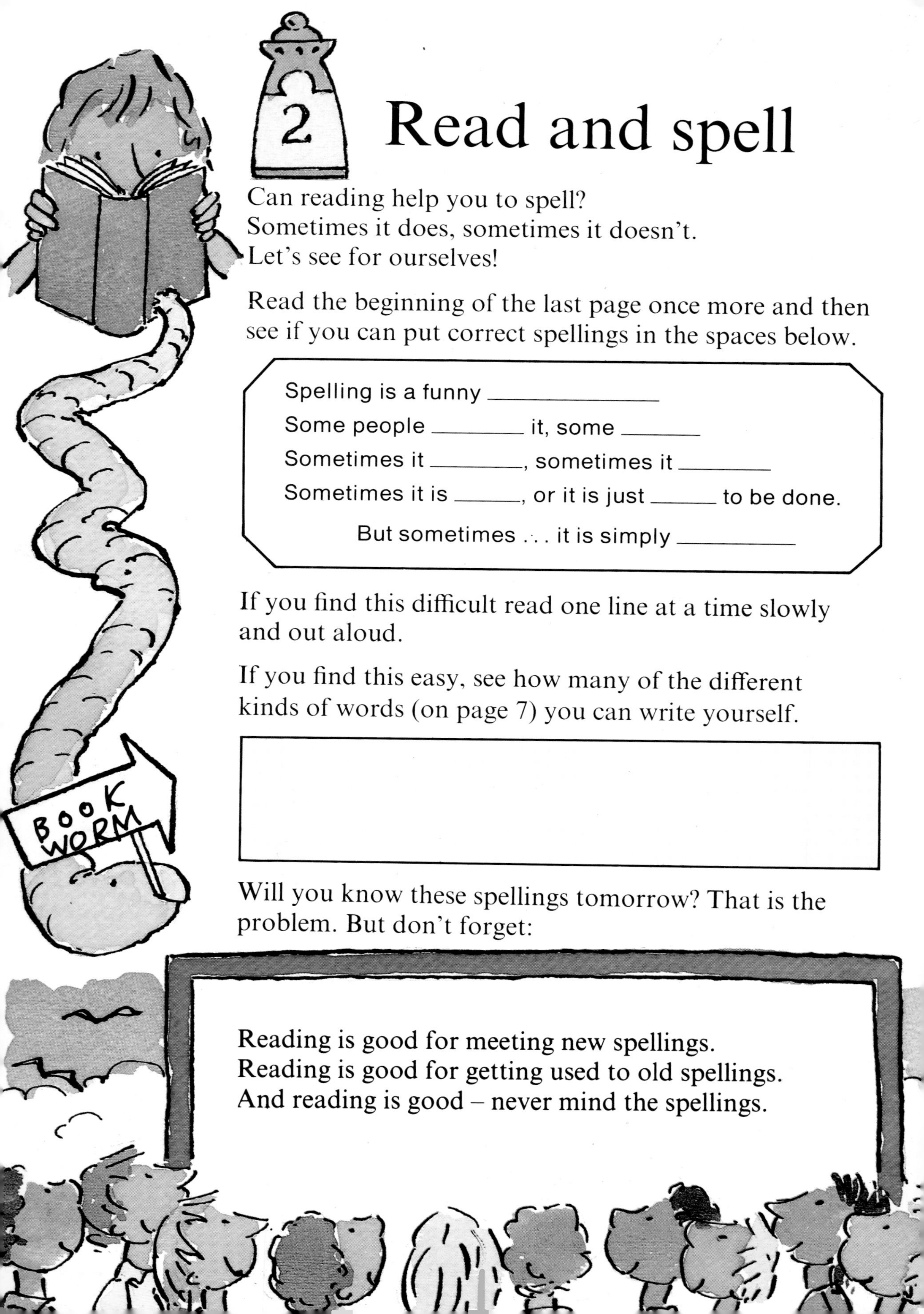

2 Read and spell

Can reading help you to spell?
Sometimes it does, sometimes it doesn't.
Let's see for ourselves!

Read the beginning of the last page once more and then see if you can put correct spellings in the spaces below.

Spelling is a funny ____________
Some people ______ it, some ______
Sometimes it ______, sometimes it ______
Sometimes it is _____, or it is just _____ to be done.
But sometimes . . . it is simply ________

If you find this difficult read one line at a time slowly and out aloud.

If you find this easy, see how many of the different kinds of words (on page 7) you can write yourself.

Will you know these spellings tomorrow? That is the problem. But don't forget:

Reading is good for meeting new spellings.
Reading is good for getting used to old spellings.
And reading is good – never mind the spellings.

But reading is a funny business too, just like spelling.

Some people love reading. They like reading fast. They like racing on with stories. They don't always look carefully at each word. They can enjoy the stories and understand every little bit without having to study the spellings. They do it almost at a glance.

Some people read slowly. They look at each word with great care and sometimes puzzle over them if they look odd. You can't help noticing the spellings if you read like this. This is how many of us start reading.

If you read aloud to yourself or a friend, then you have to read quite slowly. Saying words is different from thinking them in your head. It makes you give them each a special sound. This is useful when you start writing because you often imagine yourself talking aloud as you write.

Now read these two lines:

Once upon a time there were two talking tortoises.

Wunsapon a tym thair wer to torking tortussiz.

Which line do you find easier to read?
Do you see how good spelling makes for good reading?
Reading and spelling help each other.

So, keep on reading. If you are a fast reader and a not-very-good speller try reading a little more slowly and, if possible, aloud.

Sound and spell

. . . **found** a **shell** – **bound** to **sell**

. . . hound on **mound** – **tell** by the **smell**

The 'ound' and 'ell' parts of these words always make the same sound. The sound parts of words can help us to spell well, especially when we are first learning to write

We can all think of words with

ook sounds	or **end** sounds	or **old** sounds
cook	**lend**	**hold**
shook	**friend**	**sold**
t_____	**m**____	**t**___
_____	_____	____
_____	_____	____

Sounds are often good for helping us to get the beginnings and ends of words right.

Think of words beginning with the *b* sound.

baked beans **butterflies** **buns** **b**______ **b**______

Think of m words

mother **moon** **magic** **m**_____ **m**______ **m**__________

And think of '. . .ing' words:

singing **jumping** _______**ing** _______**ing**

A few special words can make the sounds of sounds themselves:

Making these kinds of words is called **onomatopoeia.**

But, be careful with sounds!
There are sometimes different words which sound the same:

sea see **there their** **hair hare** **to two too**

These don't look the same and nor, of course, do they mean the same thing.
These kinds of words are called **homophones.**

Then, again, there are words which can look the same but have quite different sounds and meanings. **Row,** for instance is a word you can have a **row** about when you are angry in a boat. **Lead** is another **misleading** word in this way, just like **refuse** which can be a question of obstinacy or rubbish. These kinds of words are called **homonyms**.

The letters *ough* are especially **tough** for readers because they can have so many different sounds. They come in bakers' **dough,** on a **bough** of a tree and even **through thoroughly thoughtful coughing**. In each of these words the *ough* part makes a different sound.

So you see, we cannot always depend on the sounds of words to give us the right spellings.
Sounding does help us, but it is no good without looking as well.

Look and spell

When we talk we make sounds; they are there to be heard. When we write we usually make marks on paper; they are there to be seen. To be good at writing and spelling we have to be good at seeing.

Sometimes it helps to look at words in the same way as we look at pictures.

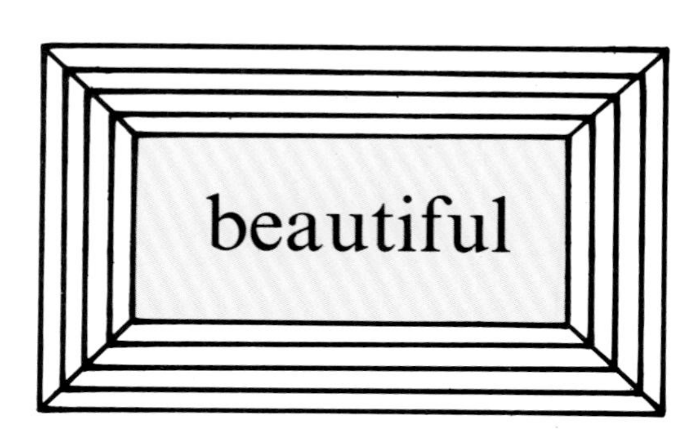

Enjoy the beauty of the shape of each letter and see how it fits together with the ones next to it to make little patterns:

bea eau tif ful

And enjoy the beauty of the shape of the whole word.

beautiful

No other word has exactly the same shape as this one. It is very special.

1. **Look** long and hard at this picture again.
2. Now **cover** it with your hand and try and see (**spell**) it in your mind.
3. Take your hand away and **check** whether the picture in your mind was the same.
4. If you were not sure try again.

LOOK ➡ COVER ➡ SPELL ➡ CHECK

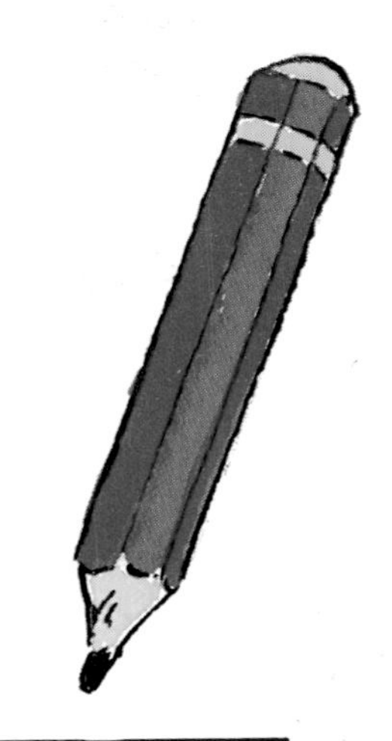

This is a very simple and useful way of helping us to spell.

Try it in turn with each of these words. *(Use a pencil in case you don't get it right first time, and, if you like, write on a separate piece of paper).*

LOOK	COVER	SPELL	CHECK
bird		bird	☒ ☑
beetle			
beard			
bear			
ear			
eye			
word		werd	
third		3rd	

Sounding does not help very much in trying to remember these words, does it? They give us an important warning:

BE WISE – USE YOUR EYES!

5 Look again and spell

The beauty of writing is that it stays. We can look at it again and again. There is always another chance to look, cover, spell and check. It does not matter how many times you keep on trying.

COKE

Sometimes a good way to start learning a new word is just to copy it letter by letter. Copy some of your favourite words into the boxes below!

Now make sure you know them:

PETS

LOOK ➡ COVER ➡ SPELL ➡ CHECK

BIRTHDAYS

HAMBURGERS

SWIMMING

BIRMINGHAM

CRISPS ~~CHOCLATE~~

Does it look right?

SKATEBOARDS

If we keep on meeting words we begin to know if they look right or not. Sometimes it helps if we try writing words in two or three different ways to see which one looks right.

busness busyness business

I ♥ ~~Spagetty~~

I ♥ ~~Spaggetty~~

I ♥ Pasta

> Can you tell which one of these looks right?
>
> **becaus becos because**
>
> **Sataday Saturday Saterday**
>
> **School scule skool**
>
> **seeling ceeling ceiling**
>
> **dissappointment disapointment disappointment**
>
> **Sepreyes surprize surprise**
>
> Check in the index if you are not sure.

Look out! Look carefully! Look again!

ICE CREAM

CHIPS

PIZZA

6 Name and spell

This book is private. Make sure that your name and address are on the inside of the front cover.

The first word that many of us learn to write is our own name. Some names are easy – **Tom**, **Pat**, **Nan** or **Ben**. Others may be not so easy – **Elizabeth**, **Christopher**, **Cecilia** or **Nebuchadnezzar**.

Names are labels: we all have to use the same ones so that we can know who, what or where we are talking or writing about. It is important to get names right. It is bad manners to call somebody or some place by the wrong name. It is also bad manners not to write a name correctly or begin it with a capital letter.

Best friends

(Write their names here on a piece of paper)

Mother	Father
1	2
3	4

Look-Cover-Spell and Check

Keep your friends – Remember their names!

PARIS is named after a Greek King's son

The right place

London   Washington   Paris   Timbuktu

Europe   Africa   America   Australia   Asia

Favourite place: ____________________

CAPITAL CAPITAL – Names of people, places and times

The right date

Days and months are tricky words. See a diary or calendar if you are not sure of any of them.

Monday
Moonday
Tuesday
TIWS day named after Saxon god
Wednesday
Wodensday named after Saxon god
Thursday
Thor's day named after Saxon god
Friday
Freya's day named after Saxon goddess
Saturday
Saturn's day named after Roman god
Sunday
named after the Sun

Do you see why **Wednesday** is not wensday?

We have to thank the Romans for the names of the months.

January February March April May June July August September October November December

Favourite Day:

Favourite Month:

JULY is named after Julius Caesar

always begin with capital letters.

Know and spell

1 Knowing words – Spelling out the meanings

Knowing the meanings of words is important for spelling. We learn meanings not just by hearing and seeing new words but especially by saying and writing them ourselves. When we do this they become *our* words with *our* meanings. By spelling them the right way we make ourselves clearly understood.

2 Knowing about words

There is a story behind the spelling of every word. English is really a mixture of words which have come from many different peoples and languages. It is a mixture which is always changing. The Saxons, the Angles, the Vikings, the Greeks, the Romans, the French and the American Indians are among the many peoples who have added words to the English language. That is why many spellings look peculiar to us now.

Greek words
drama comet medal grotto torso acrobat encyclopaedia and all those 'ology' (study of) words like psychology geology ornithology

Scottish Gaelic words
loch clan slogan whisky

Roman words
castle colonel infantry cavalry campaign.

Indian words
bungalow dungarees pyjamas curry

Welsh words
coracle flannel maggot eisteddfod

We can use some of the words that we have already met and give them special meanings of our own:

Nebuchadnezzar thought Wednesday was beautiful

Can you find ways of writing these other words in a sentence and making them yours?

Saturday **business** **tough**

or **February** **friend** **beard**

In a funny way the words with odd spellings can be the ones that most stick in our minds. See how many of these oddities stick with you. See, too, if you can make some of them your own by bringing them into a story or poem.

Italian words
piano umbrella balcony concert

German words
kindergarten hamburger pretzel plunder

French words
beef pork veal buffet café guillotine

Dutch words
golf aloof knapsack skipper yacht toy deck

Spanish words
cigar mosquito canyon rodeo alligator tornado.

American Indian words
canoe moose tepee tomahawk

You can find out more about different kinds of words in the **Kingfisher Guide to Words.**

Spell to rule

Rules are useful if they are simple and if there are not too many of them to remember. The trouble with spelling is that we can make hundreds of rules and they still don't always work.
But most good spellers keep a few rules in their mind and find that these are helpful.

So here are some rules that are often used. See which ones suit you best and which you find easiest to remember.

1 *i before e except after c – when the ie rhymes with dee*

belief, chief, pier, sieve, field, piece, ceiling, receive, receipt, deceit, conceive.
Exceptions: **weird, seize, Keith.**

2 *Watch out for suffixes – extra bits added onto the ends of words: they often change the old ending.*

[A] *y changes to i or ie, except when it is after a vowel, and not before ing.*

fly – flies, sky – skies, penalty – penalties,
happy – happily, merry – merrily,
early – earlier, ready – readiness,
day – days, boy – boys, monkey – monkeys,
Exceptions: **day – daily, portray – portrait,**
plenty – plenteous, miscellany – miscellaneous.

a e i o u are vowels

B *words ending in e drop the e when they have a suffix beginning with a vowel or a y.*

stone – stony, inquire – inquiry,
care – caring, retire – retiring,
but **careful – careless, praise – praiseworthy**
Exceptions: **argument, awful, shoeing, hoeing.**

C *Words ending in a single consonant (other than w, x or y) after a single vowel will double this consonant when there is a suffix beginning with a vowel.*

commit – committee, forget – forgetting,
fit – fitting, fitter, fittest *but* **fitness, fitful**
occur – occurrence, occurred.
Exceptions: **buses, gases, developed, developing.**

D *When full is added to a word one of the 'l's is dropped.*

care – careful, peace – peaceful, thought – thoughtful
but we always write **'... fully'** *with 2 'l's.*
carefully, peacefully, thoughtfully.

3 Watch out for plurals!

A *The usual way to make numbers of nouns is to add s to the word.*

fire – fires, boy – boys, toe – toes

B *But nouns already ending in a hissing consonant (s, sh, ch, x, z) and most nouns ending in -o add es.*

bus – buses, match – matches, box – boxes, potato – potatoes
Exceptions: **solos, pianos, banjos.**

C *Some nouns ending in f change to -ves.*

leaf – leaves, wolf – wolves *Exceptions:* **chiefs, hoofs, roofs.**

b c d f g h j k l m n p q r s t v w x y z are consonants

Compute and spell

Can computers take away the pain and strain of learning to spell? They can and they can't.

■ **Computers can correct spelling mistakes.**

Computer spell-check programs are a wonderful inventoin*. Many computers now have word-processing programs which can correct the spellings of up to 80,000 words. There could be many times when a computer with a spell-check program like this might save you a lot of bother. But there are snags, especially when we are just learning to spell.

*The spell-check will automatically change this to **invention**.

SPELL CHECK PROGRAMS

– only work if you can spell quite well already. Our guesses have to be close for the computer to recognize what we are trying to write. It might correct *sossages* but might have difficulty with *sosijiz* for *sausages*.

– cannot correct mistakes which are just wrong words as when we write *our* for *are* or *hour*, *to* for *two* or *too* and so on. It is easy to make mistakes like this and there is no way that a computer can think these ones out.

– can't check all foreign words, special invented words or unusual speech dialects like the British Cockney habit of dropping 'h's – *ave an appy new year!*

Computers can give us confidence with writing.

Writing on a computer is called word-processing.
One of the advantages of word-processing is that it can lessen the worry about spelling. With the delete key [DEL] and the cursor [→] it is easy to correct spelling mistakes without making an untidy mess. Even if you do make a spelling mistake people can think it is just a typing mistake!

Computers can help us practise looking.

Practise Look and Spell routines again.

Look – word appears on screen
Cover – word disappears from screen
Spell – you type what you remember
Check – the computer gives a signal to say if you are right or if you have to try again.

Computers can have good spelling puzzles and games.

There are many computer games and problem solving programs which directly help spelling.
Adventure games will sometimes need us to remember spellings of clues and directions. We cannot go on with the adventure or game until we have got the word right.

10 Puzzle and spell

Puzzles make us think. That's why so many of us like them, so long as they are neither too hard nor too easy. Here is some brain teasing which might help us to think in a different way about spelling.

1 Crossword.
When the words cross over each other they check the spelling.

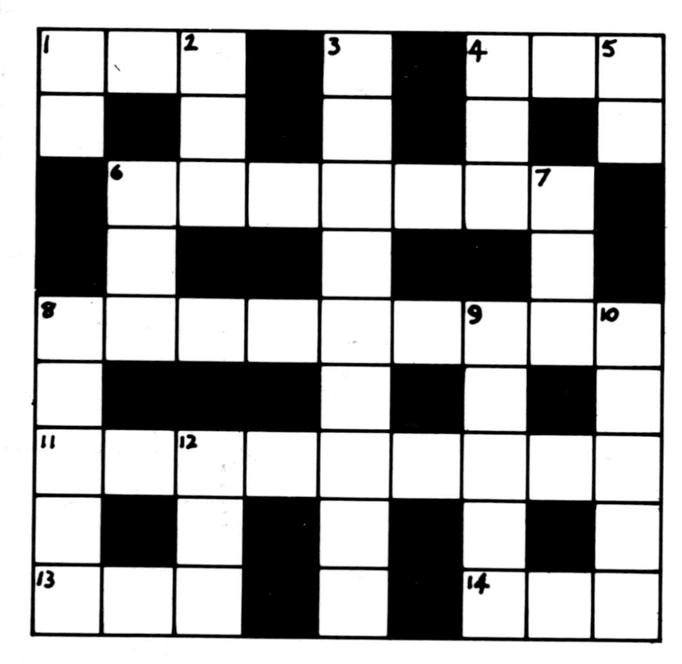

Across

1. The piper's son (3)
4. A precious stone (3)
6. (7)

8. Something said in anger (9)
11. (9)

13. What we breathe (3)
14. A large tree (3)

Down

1. . . . and fro (2)
2. Part of a Scottish name (3)
3. Puzzle like this (9)
4. A kind of antelope (3)
5. Myself (2)
6. Used for rowing (3)
7. Male teacher or knight (3)
8. Warm milky drink (5)
9. Girl or tree (5)
10. A sleep story (5)
12. Belonging to us (4)

2 A rebus rhyme

YYUR
YYUB
ICUR
YY4me.
(How should this rhyme really be written?)

3 Hidden animals
Can you see the animal hidden in each sentence?

(a) He came looking for trouble.
(b) They can be espied around the blossom.
(c) Impossible! O pardon me.
(d) Up I go.
(e) Well, I only got terrified out of my wits.
(2 animals)

4 Palindromes
What is the same about these names?

ANNA BOB ADA HANNAH

And what is peculiar about these sentences?

Madam I'm Adam.
God! a dog!
Step on no pets.

5 Anagram countries
(a) Erin lad
(b) Rain
(c) A tiger Ann
(d) Lop Dan
(e) Flan din
(f) Ada can

6 Mixed bags
See how many words you can make out of this mixed bag of letters.

m i x e d b a g

7 Mixed bags
See how many words you can make out of this mixed bag of word pieces.

o pen to ed call car cil win e ful ly bar w do sh s less hop and at here

8 Food Chain
Sausageggsugaradish
(See how long you can make it)

Invent and spell

The key to all learning

★ Babies learn to talk by inventing words and new ways of saying them. They soon grow out of it but they have to start by finding out for themselves.

★ Young children often invent pretend-writing before they go to school. It makes them feel good and helps them to know what writing is about.

★ Spelling, too, has to begin with a lot of inventing. How can we possibly know it all before we begin?

Even when we are quite good at spelling there are still times when we have to invent or guess. Our invention might not be correct but it is often better to have a go than to wait for someone else to show us. Making mistakes is an important part of learning.

Sometimes our inventions can be **crazy** –

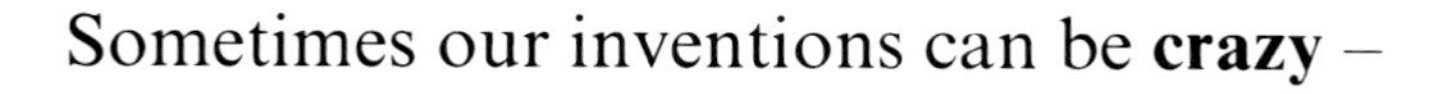

krehsee *craysy* *creyzi*

Making different crazy spellings can be fun and can sometimes help us to think about ways of spelling. Think of other crazy spellings for these words.

lunatic **daft** **amazing** **unbelievable**

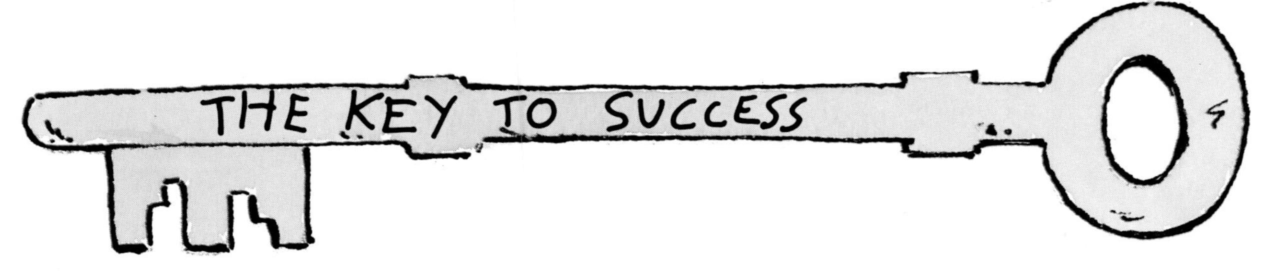

Complete inventions

Here are some new animals. Can you invent names for them? Maybe you can also make up the sounds that they make.

Whatever you **write** will be **right**. You invented these names and sounds yourself. These are the spellings which everybody else will now have to use for these creatures!

Getting it right

★ Good inventors know that with perseverance our inventions will get *beta* and *betta* and **better**.

★ Good inventors know that in the end they need to have good manners to make people notice their inventions. This means correct spellings. They make people think that you and your writing are important.

12 Search and spell

Dear Reader,

I have something to tell you. Actually, I am not brilliant at spelling myself. If I didn't have two dictionaries beside me and a patient wife who could answer all my questions I would not have been able to write this book.

They have been wonderful. With their help I can now be certain that all the spellings are correct – except for the funny inventing bits. (I still can't be sure of remembering Nebuchadnezzar – thank goodness I haven't got a friend called that!)

I thought you ought to know my secret.

Yours sincerely,

William Edmonds.

Hooray for Dictionaries!

Nearly every writer has a dictionary or two. Some writers use dictionaries to check spellings and meanings much more than others. It's their business. Nobody minds.

Dictionaries come in many different sizes and kinds.

Which one

Small dictionaries are useful for finding everyday spellings and meanings. Sometimes they have pictures to show the meanings of words. They are good for checking words which can easily be confused –

horse *n* a four-legged animal with hooves . . .
hoarse *adj.* of the voice, rough or croaking.

or the right place/plaice

place *n* a particular area or location.
plaice *n* a kind of flat fish.

When

Sometimes it is best to do all your writing quickly while the ideas are in your head and then check the spelling afterwards. Or sometimes it is best to use a dictionary as you write.

How

Dictionaries are good for making us concentrate on the order of letters in a word. Alphabetical order is a good way of sorting out words. Can you put these words in the order in which you find them in the dictionary?

adjective achieve after alligator
acrobat adverb accommodation aloof

Check the first words in the index to see whether your order is correct.

Remember and spell

One of the oldest ways of trying to remember spellings is to make lists and then learn the list by heart. When you think you have learned each list – maybe looking > covering > spelling > checking each word as you go along – get somebody to test you. This is a way that teachers often like to train our memories. It can be a good way of doing a little at a time – say a list or a half-list every day.

IMPORTANT

Make sure you choose or make a list that is right for you. It must be neither impossibly difficult nor too easy.

Here are a few lists for you to try. As you see there are many different ways of making groups of words. You can try and make some more.

starters	shopping	rhymes
good	sugar	fat
food	eggs	cat
get	biscuits	sat
wet	jam	flat
sad	honey	that
lad	bread	rat
bed	milk	spat
said	coffee	gnat

'pp's	teasers	homophones
pepper	knee	sale
stopped	key	sail
shopping	knife	piece
kipper	comb	peace
slipper	bomb	their
happy	gnome	there
disappointment	tongue	wood
apparatus	sign	would

'ough's	specials	story words
although	accommodation	once
cough	answer	upon
bought	because	there
brought	especially	was
through	mysterious	ugly
thorough	necessary	princess
thought	occur	happily
enough	unusual	after

?	'qu's	words from Greek
Who	quiet	alphabet
Why	quite	comet
When	squash	xylophone
How	square	telephone
Where	inquiry	geography
What	queen	archaeology
Whose	request	biology
Which	question	psychology

'i's & 'e's	extras	private specials
ceiling	exciting	
sieve	exaggerate	______________
niece	extraordinary	
achieve	excellent	______________
field	exercise	
receive	expensive	______________
deceit	extravagant	
friend	exquisite	______________

Fed up with testing? Why not try writing little nonsense rhymes or stories using some of the lists? It may be an even better way of remembering them.

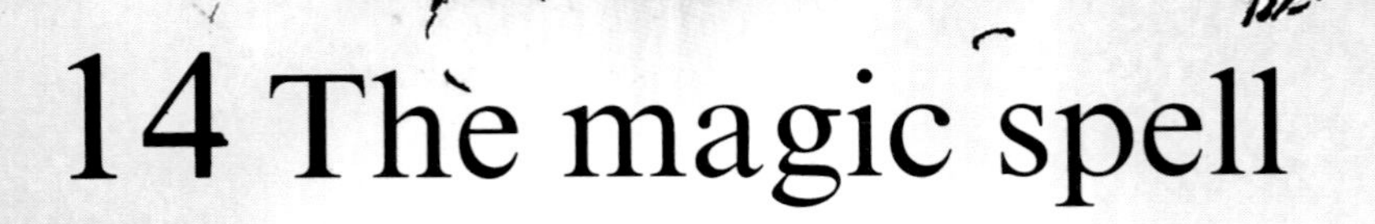

14 The magic spell

Take each of the ingredients and taste them one by one before putting them in the pot.
Add some extra portions of the ones you particularly like.
Then slowly stir the whole mixture.

Let it brew!
Let the smell enter your nostrils!
Let the colours fill your eyes!
Let the hissing fill your ears!
Let the thoughts fill your mind!
Let the spell take its time!

Then *write* and *write* and *write*!

GOOD WORDS

The Treasures

Words

Words are Wonderful

We speak with words
and we listen to words.

We write words
and we read words.

And we think with words.

We humans are so lucky. We are the only creatures on earth to have such wonderful treasures:

✻ Words as tools
Words are tools which we use to communicate with each other. We use them to talk, discuss, argue, agree, describe, plan, organize, remember, sing, imagine and do all manner of things to help us live and thrive.

✻ Words as jewels
When we take care to choose just the right words they become like glittering jewels. They are a great pleasure to listen to and read. Everybody wants to know what they are about.

This A to Z guide is like a small treasure chest. Open it and you will find 40 different kinds of word, including all the important 'parts of speech' (marked by a *).

BE WARNED! Good words are impossible to resist.

□ Abbreviations

An abbreviation is a short way of writing a word or group of words. Sometimes it is just a part of a full word. Sometimes it is made up of initial letters.

Thomas

* Some kinds of abbreviations are used by everybody:

Titles:	Names	Countries
Mr for mister	*Tom* for Thomas	*U.K. (G.B.)*
Mrs for missus	*Ben* for Benjamin	*U.S.A.*
Col. for colonel	*Pat* for Patricia	*U.S.S.R.*

Patricia

Several words, like *phone, photo, maths, TV* are better known as abbreviations than in their full form.

A few English abbreviations come from other languages:
RSVP for 'repondez s'il vous plaît' – French for *please reply.*
NB for 'nota bene' – Latin for *note well.*
AD for Anno Domini – Latin for *in the year of the Lord.*

Benjamin

* Other kinds of abbreviations are ones that we make for ourselves or use just with people that we know. They can be a kind of slang like *brill* for brilliant or *telly* for television.

> Have you any good abbreviations for the names of your friends?

□ Acronyms

An acronym is a kind of abbreviation. It is a word formed from the initial or first letters of a group of other words.

*LASER (***L**ight **A**mplification by **S**timulated **E**mission of **R**adiation)
RADAR (**RA**dio **D**etection **A**nd **R**anging)
SCUBA (**S**elf-**C**ontained **U**nderwater **B**reathing **A**pparatus)

Angry, awkward cats

Beautiful, black cats

Cheeky, cheerful cats

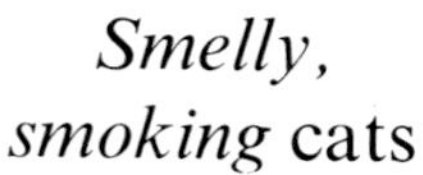

Smelly, smoking cats

□ Adjectives*

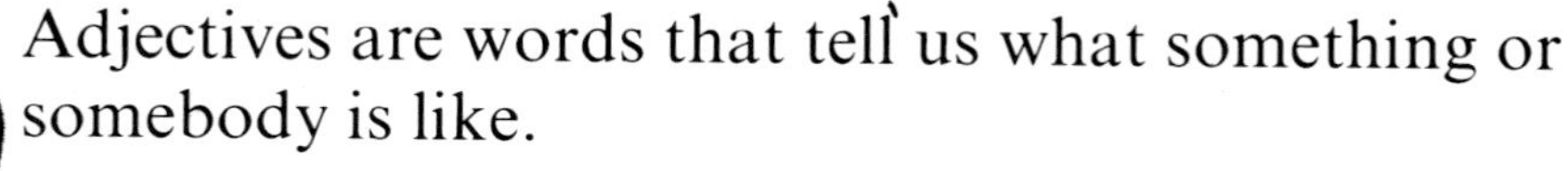

Adjectives are words that tell us what something or somebody is like.

Did you know, for instance, that there were so many different kinds of cat?

These words about cats are all being used as adjectives, although sometimes they can be used as other parts of speech. *Zoo* and *jelly*, for instance, are better known as **nouns**, but occasionally, as here, we can use nouns as adjectives. Also we can make certain verbs into adjectives: cats that lie down and watch out can become *lying* and *watchful* cats.

Zoo cats

How about making an A to Z of adjectives for something else that you like: kinds of people, days, houses, ideas or whatever?

Watchful, wily cats

Vicious, vigorous cats

Ugly, undesirable cats

Young, yellow cats

Excellent cats

Tame, tabby cats

Quiet, queenly cats

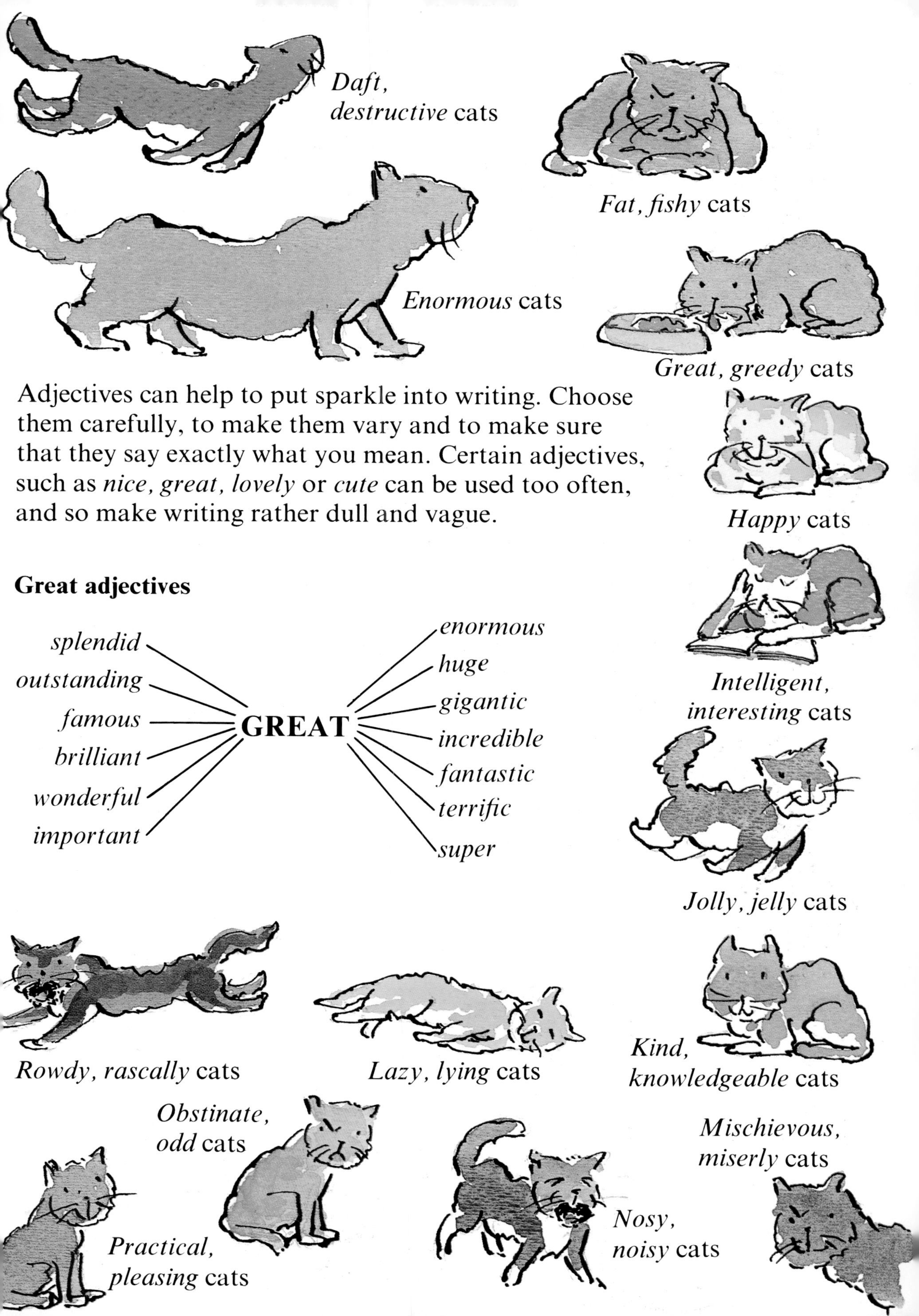

Adjectives can help to put sparkle into writing. Choose them carefully, to make them vary and to make sure that they say exactly what you mean. Certain adjectives, such as *nice, great, lovely* or *cute* can be used too often, and so make writing rather dull and vague.

Great adjectives

□ Adverbs*

An adverb is a word which tells you *how* something is done, whether, for instance, it is done *quickly, efficiently, neatly, badly* or *well*. It adds to a verb.

There are many ways of walking: *fast, slowly, backwards, stupidly, stiffly, purposefully, lightly, thoughtfully, carelessly* or *dangerously*.

"And there are many ways of talking,"
she said *very loudly*.
"No need to shout,"
he answered *coolly*.
"I thought you were deaf,"
she added *angrily*.
"No, I can hear you *perfectly well*,"
he said *politely*.
"Well, I was going to say that
we need to use adverbs to
be clear about the different ways
of talking or shouting,"
she finished *more calmly*.

> Select (*jokingfully*, if you like) some adverbs for different ways of eating, writing, singing or driving.

Adverbs can often be made out of adjectives: the cats played *awkwardly, cheekily,* and so on.
They can answer the questions When? Where? How? How often? and so on.
Adverbs may also add to adjectives or other adverbs:

very beautiful,
amazingly handsome
or *unspeakably, revoltingly* ugly.

amazingly
handsome

□ Antonyms

An antonym is a word which is opposite in meaning to another word.

long – short
clever – stupid
enemy – friend
safe – dangerous

difficult – easy
shallow – deep
fast – slow
huge – tiny

Sometimes an antonym can be made by adding a **prefix** such as *un-* or *dis-*

kind – unkind
do – undo

like – dislike
appear – disappear

Antonyms can help us to think clearly about the meanings of words and, just occasionally, they can be a good test of the imagination.

□ Articles*

As well as being things or pieces of writing, articles are particular kinds of words, ones that introduce other words.

There is the **definite article:** *the*.
The definite article is so called because when we use it we are definite about which one we mean – the article in the newspaper has to be one particular article.

And there is the **indefinite article:** *a* or *an*.
The indefinite article is so called because we are not definite about what is being referred to – an article in a newspaper could mean any old article from anywhere.

It is important to take care in choosing which indefinite article to use – *a* or *an*.

a comes before words beginning with consonants.
an goes before words beginning with vowels (*a e i o u*).

an amazing rabbit – *a* white rabbit

☐ Beautiful words

crocodile, snooker, exquisite, anaconda, O, marmalade.
marigold, indigo, glorious, cinnamon, extravaganza,

Beautiful words are really a matter of personal taste.

Can you name and frame some which you think are really beautiful?

☐ Borrowed Words

Many English words are borrowed from other languages. Here are a few to show how world-wide the borrowing has been:

automatic (Greek)
banana (West African)
curry (Tamil)
pyjamas (Hindu)
gingham (Malay)
hamburger (German)
judo (Japanese)
khaki (Urdu)
limerick (Irish)
mattress (Arabic)
piano (Italian)
robot (Czech)
safari (Swahili)
tea (Chinese)
ukelele (Hawaiian)
vodka (Russian)
yacht (Dutch)
zebra (Bantu)

☐ Brief words

We say that we have had a brief word with someone when we mean we have had a short conversation. That's all.

There are over 30 two-letter words in the English language. How many can you write?

□ Common confusions

Here are a few pairs of almost similar words which often cause confusion:

affect ***effect***	In the common use of these words *affect* is a verb (Smoking may *affect* your health) and *effect* is a noun (Smoking can have dangerous *effects* on your health).
complement ***compliment***	*Complement* means to fill out to make whole; *compliment* means to praise.
disinterested ***uninterested***	*Disinterested* means being impartial, unbiased. *Uninterested* suggests a lack of all interest.
emigrate ***immigrate***	*Emigrate* means to move to another country; *immigrate* means to come from another country.
principal ***principle***	*Principal* can be a noun meaning chief (She is *principal* of a college) or an adjective (My *principal* reason is . . .). *Principle* is only a noun and means a fundamental belief (I refuse on *principle*).
stationery ***stationary***	*Stationery* refers to writing materials whereas *stationary* means staying still.

The best way of checking words which are easily confused is to use a good dictionary.

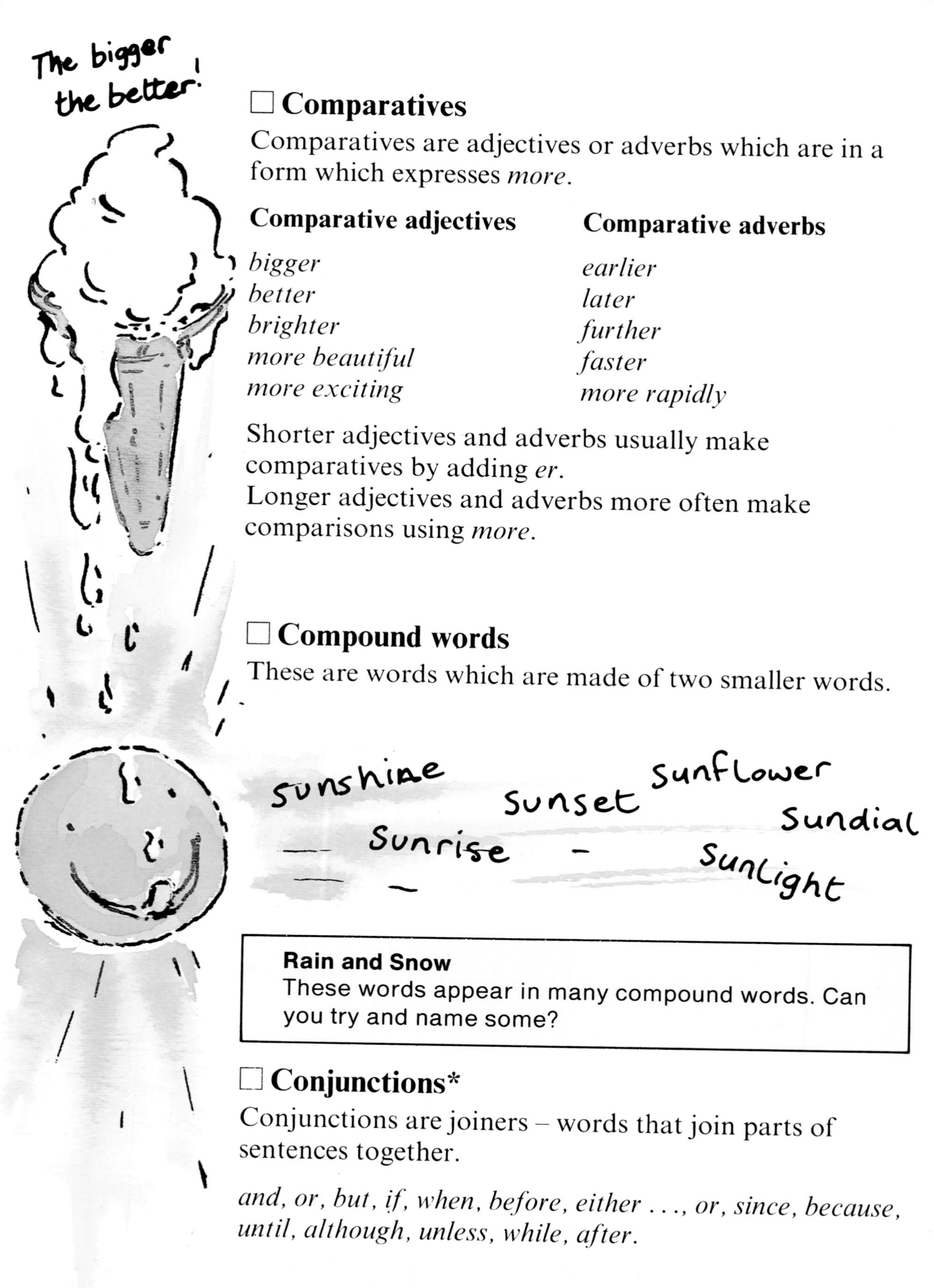

☐ Comparatives

Comparatives are adjectives or adverbs which are in a form which expresses *more*.

Comparative adjectives	**Comparative adverbs**
bigger	*earlier*
better	*later*
brighter	*further*
more beautiful	*faster*
more exciting	*more rapidly*

Shorter adjectives and adverbs usually make comparatives by adding *er*.
Longer adjectives and adverbs more often make comparisons using *more*.

☐ Compound words

These are words which are made of two smaller words.

> **Rain and Snow**
> These words appear in many compound words. Can you try and name some?

☐ Conjunctions*

Conjunctions are joiners – words that join parts of sentences together.

and, or, but, if, when, before, either . . ., or, since, because, until, although, unless, while, after.

☐ Contractions

Contractions are words which are combined and then shortened by taking out one or more letters. The place of the missing letters is usually filled with an apostrophe (').

<table>
<tr><td colspan="3">n't (not)

can't (cannot), couldn't (could not), don't, doesn't, didn't, hasn't. wouldn't, couldn't, won't, (will not).</td><td colspan="3">'d (had, would)

he'd (he would or he had), we'd, I'd, you'd, they'd.</td></tr>
<tr><td colspan="2">'ll (will)

he'll (he will), I'll and so on.</td><td colspan="2">'ve (have)

I've (I have), we've (we have).</td><td colspan="2">'re (are)

We're (we are).</td></tr>
<tr><td colspan="6">'s (is, has)

she's (she is, or she has) and it's (it is) – not to be confused with its with no apostrophe, meaning belonging to it.</td></tr>
</table>

It is often the case that we use contractions more when we talk than when we write. If you are not sure which form to use, or want to be formal and polite, it is probably best to use the full words.

☐ Diminutives

Diminutives are words that indicate smaller versions of things or creatures.

booklet, piglet, duckling, kitchenette, hillock, miniskirt.

They are usually made by adding **suffixes** (*-let, -ling, -et, -ette, -kin, -ock*) or the **prefix** *mini*.

The young of animals give rise to a lot of special names:

chicks Puppies Spry cygnets cubs
kittens bunnies elvers leverets

Tadpoles
owlets
fawns
foals
calves
Lambs

☐ Euphemisms

Euphemisms are words which make some things seem a little more pleasant or more easy to accept than if a more direct word was used.

Passing away is a euphemism sometimes used for dying. *Toilet* (originally meaning 'getting dressed and made up') or *lavatory* (originally meaning 'a washing place or vessel') are words that have many other euphemisms: *convenience, WC* (*water closet*), *Gentlemen, Gents, Ladies, cloakroom, bathroom, restroom* and so on.

Not very nice
This can be a euphemism for all kinds of words and expressions. Perhaps you can suggest ways of being blunt and direct about something you don't approve of.

☐ Exclamations

These are words which exclaim, so as to show warning, surprise, urgency, horror, disappointment and so on.

☐ Expletives

These are kinds of **exclamations** which are used for expressing really strong feelings of disgust, frustration, sudden pain or anger.

Ouch!　　Bother!

Eek!　　Damnation

☐ Exploding words

EXPLOSION

BAAAAANG!

CRRRAAAASSSSSH!

Now explode these words: *ATTISHOO!*　　*SPLASH!*

☐ Happy Words

Happiness is . . . . Can you describe a truly happy moment of your own?

□ Homonyms

A homonym (taken from two Greek words: *homo* – meaning same – and *nym* – meaning name) is a word which has one spelling but more than one meaning. Here are examples:

coach, match, race, ram, saw, stamp, tie, watch.

Homonyms are often found in riddles.

1 Why are rivers handy places for collecting money?

2 When is a guilty person like a firework?

3 Why are waiters good at sums?

Watch
Watch!

> **1** Because they have *banks* on either side.
> **2** When they can both be *let off*.
> **3** Because they know their *tables*.

□ Homophones

A homophone (taken from the Greek words meaning *same* and *sound*) is a word which has the same sound as another word but has a different spelling.

fair/fare, meet/meat, there/their, see/sea.

These kinds of words can easily cause confusion with spelling. They can also lead to clever double meanings and funny jokes.

> Do you know about the three sons who took over a cattle ranch from their father? They called it Focus because it is where *the sun's rays meet/the sons raise meat*.

do you have trouble with the hare on your hair?

Jokes and riddles using homophones are best when they are told and not just read. This kind of word play is known as making a pun. Puns often come to *sighs/size*!

□ Imperatives

Imperatives are words which are used for giving orders. They are verbs used in a basic form (infinitive without the 'to').

Be quiet!

Will you please *do* as you are told at once!

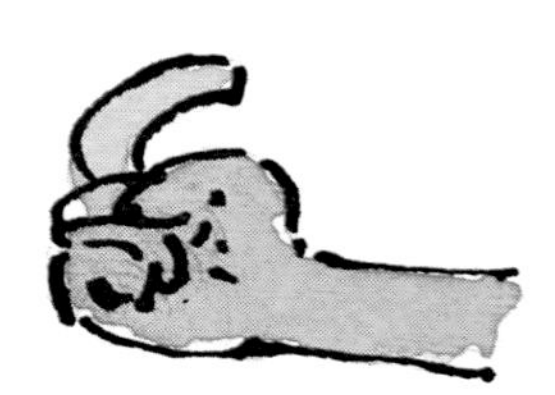

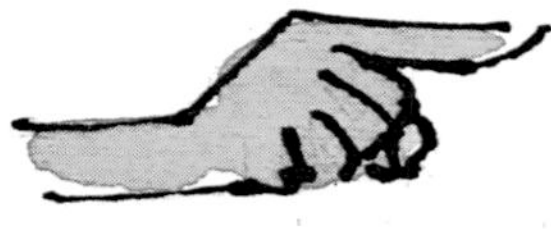

Come here!

Stop that horrible noise!

Listen to me!

Don't do that any more!

Children often have to put up with hearing imperatives.

> What are some of the favourite imperatives used by your parents or teachers?

□ Interrogatives*

These are words which introduce questions.

Why is there so much salt in the sea?
Where is the Sargasso Sea?
How did the world begin?
Who invented toothpaste?
When will pigs learn to fly?

> *Why* oh *why*? Why not ask a few questions yourself about pigs, planets, people or whatever?

☐ Journalese

Journalese refers to the kinds of words that journalists like to use in newspapers.
They like their writing to be 'punchy', using simple words in a way which is dramatic and eye-catching.

Children hit by Teachers' strike
SHOPKEEPER SLAMS COUNCIL
THIEVES GEM SNATCH

☐ Kennings

Kennings are unusual descriptions which are used in place of names. They are often like riddles.

goggle box (T.V.) Adam's ale (water)
ship of the desert (camel)

Goggle box
Four stiff standers
Four dilly danders
Two lookers
Two crookers
And a wig wag
4 legs,
4 teats,
2 eyes,
2 horns
and a tail

☐ Nouns*

Nouns are naming words. We use them to label anything that can be seen, heard or thought. You name it – it's a noun.

Nouns have a kind of magic power. When we speak or write a noun we can conjure up a picture of it in our mind. Nouns let us talk, write or think about anything we like without having to have it around.

* We can whet our appetite by looking at all the nouns on a menu.

* We can make lists of nouns to be bought from the shops.

Menu
1
steak
Sausages
bacon
Hamburger
CHIPS
lemonade
Coke
Ice cream
chocolate
Vanilla
Strawberry
Sugar
eggs
Jam
honey
bread
milk
Coffee
peanut butter

* We can check time nouns on a calendar.

* We can collect nouns from all around us: in the kitchen, in the bedroom, in the cupboard, under the floorboards, outside in the garden, in the street, in the countryside, at sea, in the sky, in space or just in the head.

The Kitchen
cooker, fridge, knife, fork, bowl, plate, cloth, sink, butter, eggs, floor, mess . . .

Collect some nouns for your bedroom or other places that you like,

* We can play games with nouns.

I spy with my little eye . . .

* We can use nouns to make stories.

Once upon a time there was a beautiful .... (**common noun**). She was called .... (**proper noun**). She lived in a .... (**c.n.**) near a .... (**c.n.**).

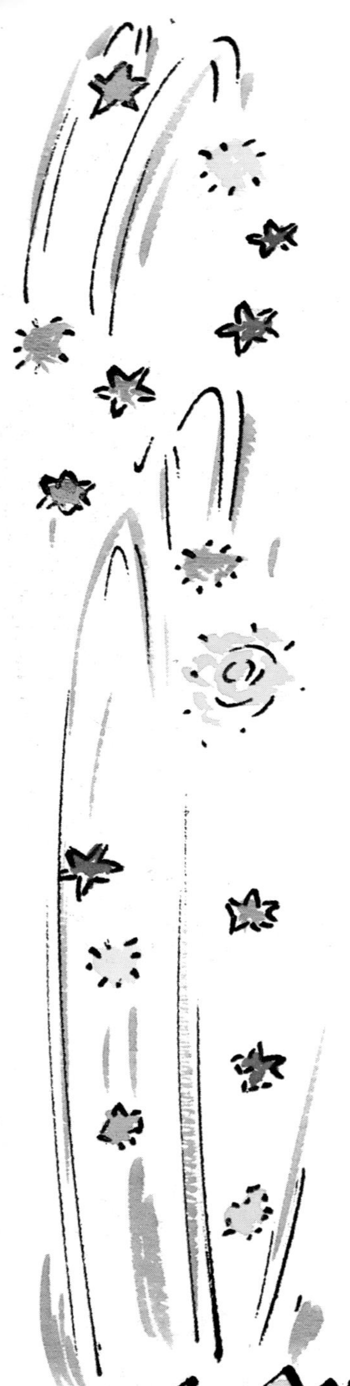

☐ Noun groups*

Proper nouns: those which name particular people, animals, places and times. They always begin with capital letters.

Mary Jones and *Spot* (the dog) at *Birmingham* on *Friday*.

Common nouns: those which name the kind of person, etc. rather than naming a particular one. They can be concrete nouns, abstract nouns or collective nouns.

Concrete nouns are the names of anything that can actually be seen or touched.

cabbages, kings, computers, cogs, helicopters, hedgehogs.

Abstract nouns are the names of anything that can only be thought about and not seen or touched.

wind, noise, happiness, poverty, honesty, idea.

Collective nouns are used to name a collection of creatures or things.

a herd of cows
a gaggle of geese
a pack of wolves
a clump of trees
a company of actors
a flock of sheep
a pride of lions
a pack of cards
a swarm of bees
a gang of thieves

Sometimes it is fun to make up collective nouns of one's own, how about:

A crackle of Fireworks

A talkshop of teachers

A spin of spiders

What might be good collective nouns for helicopters, hedgehogs, or ghosts?

□ Personal Words

A few words are taken from the names of people who first invented or used something.

Hooligan
This is taken from the name, Houlihan, the head of an Irish family who lived in London and were well known for their noisy and unruly behaviour.

Wellington boots
These were named after the Duke of Wellington, a British general, who wore knee-high riding boots specially made for him.

Lord *Sandwich,* Giuseppi *Garibaldi,* Charles *Mackintosh,* Daniel *Fahrenheit,* Ladilao *Biro* and Lord *Cardigan* also had their names given to things which we all know about today, even if we have forgotten about the people.

How about inventing something to be named after your own name?

□ Prefixes

A prefix is that part of a word which is sometimes added (fixed) at the beginning.

pre- (meaning *before*) is the prefix of prefix, prehistoric, and predict.

un- (not or reverse) as in unhappy, untidy, undo, unwind.

mis- (wrong) as in mistake, mispell, misapply, misdeed.

a-, fore-, co- (with), *circum-* (around), *semi-* (half), *re-* (again), *super-* (above), *trans-* (across), *ob-* (against), *poly-* (many), *tele-* (from afar), and *vice-* (in place of) are among the common prefixes. Many of them come from Latin and Greek words.

Autosuggestion (self-suggestion)
How many *auto-* words can you yourself suggest?

Co–
star
operate
incidental
habit
here
education

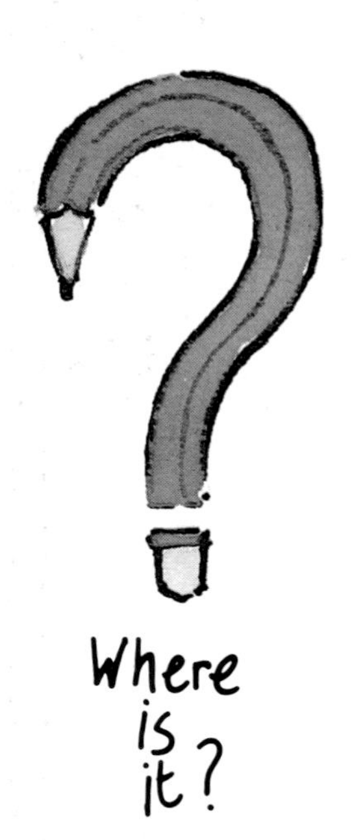

☐ Prepositions*

A preposition is a word which tells where something is in relation to something else.

Where is the missing pencil?
Is it *in* the living room, *on* the floor, *by* the television, *over* there, *under* the newspaper, *with* the other pencils, *in front of* you, *behind* you, *up on* the shelf, *out of* reach, *down* there, *through* the hall or is it *right beside* you?

> **Directions**
> See how many different prepositions you can use to describe the way *to* your nearest post office.

☐ Pronouns*

What's all this about YOU and me?

Pronouns are words used in place of nouns. There are really five kinds of pronouns.

Personal pronouns
I, you, he, she, it, we, they, me, him, her, us, them.

Relative pronouns
who, whose, whom, which, that.

Possessive pronouns
mine, yours, his, hers, its, ours, theirs.

Interrogative pronouns
What? Who? Which? Whom? Whose?

Demonstrative pronouns
this, these, that, those.

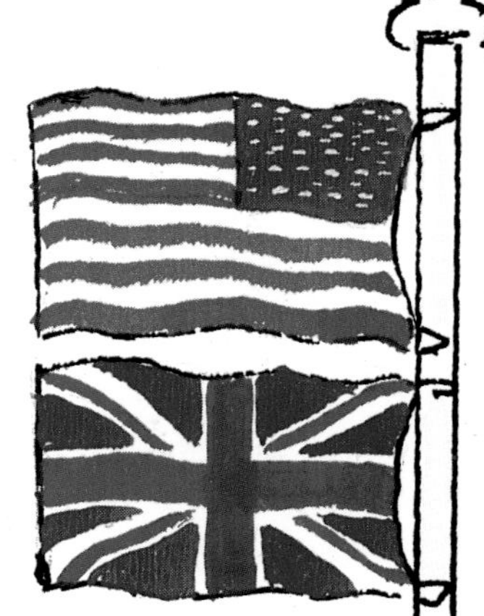

□ Regional Words

These refer to English words that particular countries or regions keep as their own. We can see this, for instance, in some of the differences between British and North American words, or between Australian and British words.

American	British
apartment	flat
closet	cupboard
cookies	biscuits
elevator	lift
fall	autumn
faucet	tap
gas(olene)	petrol
sidewalk	pavement

Australian	British
creek	stream
outback	countryside
paddock	(any) field
squatter	farmer
whinge	complain

These are good examples of how words can change from place to place and from time to time. They demonstrate the richness of the English language.

□ Slang

Slang is the name given to words which we like to use when talking with people we know. They are not usually regarded as acceptable for serious conversation or for writing. Common slang words change with fashion.

Certain words such as idiot, money, clever and good have a lot of substitute slang words.

Idiot *wally, burk, goon, twit, noodle.*

Money *dough, smackers, greens, readies.*

Clever *brainy, egghead.*

Good *magic, smashing, ace, brilliant, groovy.*

What is the latest slang that you have heard for these words?

Enjoy
Enjoyable
Endings!

☐ Suffixes

A suffix is that part of a word which is sometimes added (fixed) at the end – a word ending. If you understand about suffixes you can use them to build up thousands of words.

With *-able, -al, -age,* and *-an* we can change the words enjoy, music, marry, suburb into *enjoyable, musical, marriage, suburban.*

-ary, -ate, -ess (for female forms) as in actress and tigress), *-ful, -fy, -ish, -ism, -ity, -less, -ment* and *-ness* are among the many common suffixes.

> Effortless Cleverness
> Try making adjectives turn into abstract nouns by adding *-ness, goodness* ...
> And try making nouns turn into adjectives by adding *-less, mindless* ...

only the best

☐ Superlatives

Superlatives are adjectives or adverbs which are in a form which expresses *most*.

Superlative adjectives	**Superlative adverbs**
biggest	*latest*
best	*soonest*
worst	*most disgustingly*
most difficult	*most fortunately*

☐ Syllables

A syllable is a section or part of a word which can be said by itself.

Ambulance has three syllables: *am-bu-lance*
Good has only one syllable: *good*
Examination has five: *ex-am-in-a-tion.*

☐ Synonyms

A synonym is a word which has the same meaning as another one.

quick – fast, annually – yearly, vacant – empty

A Thesaurus is a book which provides an alphabetical list of words with their synonyms. Using synonyms is a way of avoiding tedious repetition of one word and therefore of helping to make your writing more interesting.

☐ Tongue Twisters

These are words deliberately placed together to make them difficult to speak out aloud without twisting the tongue in knots.

I miss my Swiss, my Swiss miss misses me.
I miss the bliss that Swiss kiss gives to me.

A tutor who tooted the flute
Tried to tutor two tooters to toot.
Said the two to the tutor:
Is it harder to toot, or
To tutor two tooters to toot?

□ Verbs*

Verbs are 'doing' words. They are the words that show something happening or being. Verbs bring nouns to life.

Take an apple pie. It *is* not very interesting unless you *can do* something with it. But, as a very old English rhyme *tells* us, all sorts of things *can happen* to it if we *put* some verbs before it.

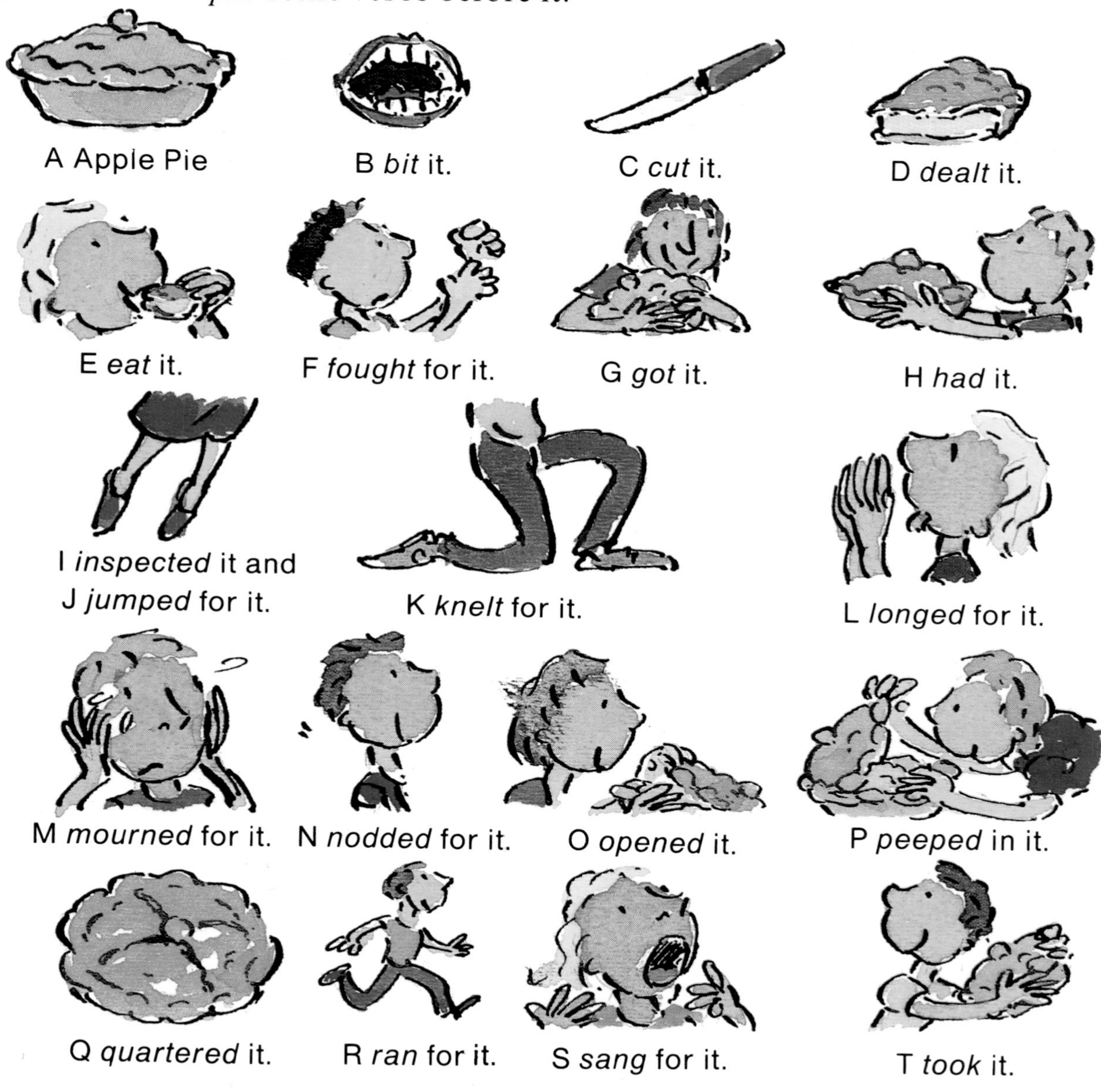

A Apple Pie
B *bit* it.
C *cut* it.
D *dealt* it.
E *eat* it.
F *fought* for it.
G *got* it.
H *had* it.
I *inspected* it and
J *jumped* for it.
K *knelt* for it.
L *longed* for it.
M *mourned* for it.
N *nodded* for it.
O *opened* it.
P *peeped* in it.
Q *quartered* it.
R *ran* for it.
S *sang* for it.
T *took* it.

UVWXYZ all *had* a slice and *went* off to bed.

Verbs are the key part of any sentence. A group of words *cannot make* a sentence unless it has at least one verb.

The black cat ________________ the fish.

We could put many different words in this gap to make the whole part into a sentence: *licked, liked, pawed, sniffed, gobbled, spat at,* and *ate*.

Each verb can also change into many different tenses:
present – *eats* or *is eating,*
past – *was eating, ate, has eaten,* or *had eaten.*
future – *is going to eat, will eat.*
conditional – *would eat, would have eaten.*
And, of course, they can have negatives: *is not eating, did not eat, won't eat,* etc.

> The lion .... the mouse. You .... them.
> Can you *bring* these pairs of nouns and pronouns alive with verbs and other words?

As they say:

replied
murmured
shouted
interrupted
said
asked
jeered
cried
hissed
exclaimed

☐ Wise words

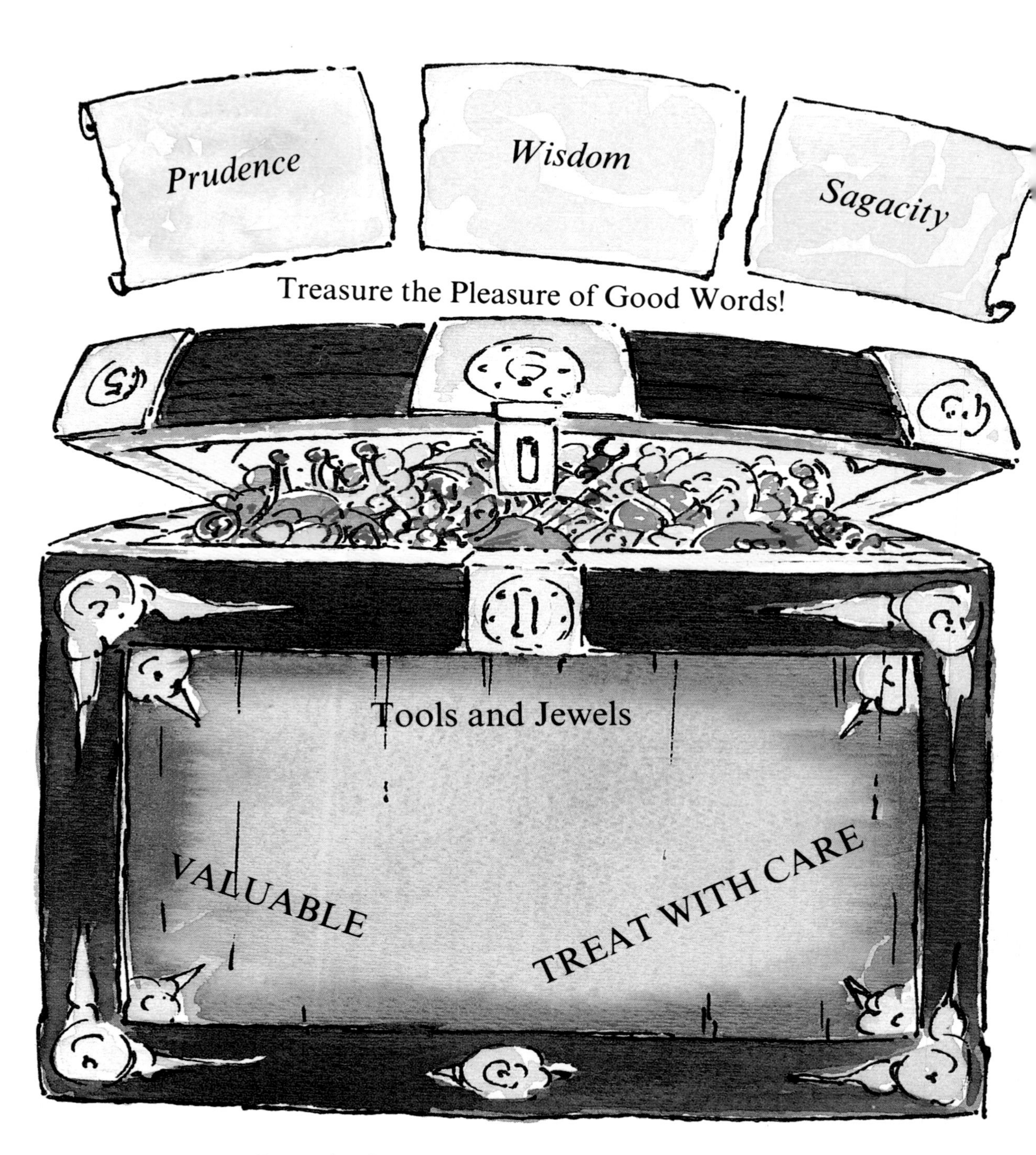

Be wise!
Write, write and *write!*

GOOD GRAMMAR

Order of Appearance
Good Grammar – Skill and Thrill
page 66
The making of grammar
Talking sense
page 68
Writing just right
page 69
Reading for meaning
page 70
The working of grammar
Sentence breaking
page 72
Sentence building
page 74
Sentence joining
page 83
Sentence extending
page 84
Sentence punctuating
page 86
Sentence style
page 88
Sentence translation
page 89
Sentence checking
page 90
Sentence sense
page 92
Index
page 126

Good Grammar – Skill and Thrill

(Jumbled-up words are difficult to read and understand. Do you see what we mean?)

That is why we have grammar – a way of arranging words into sentences so that they make sense for everybody.

We all love good grammar. Saying things the right way makes for funny jokes, fascinating gossip, pleasant conversations, exciting stories, interesting information, lively arguments, special secrets, enjoyable entertainment and all kinds of fun with words. Like juggling, grammar can be exciting and skilful. We can use it to make words do almost anything we like.

Learning good grammar

Learning the skills of good grammar is much easier than most of us realize. It happens in two main ways.

1 Making our own Grammar

We find ourselves making grammar all the time that we try to talk, read or write. We do it quite naturally and without first learning any rules. We want to make sense for ourselves and to fit in with the language we hear and see around us. We do this almost automatically.

2 Looking at how Grammar Works

This means looking at how sentences really work. It means breaking them apart and building them up so as to see how different kinds of words do different jobs. It means seeing how different parts of sentences fit together, and how different kinds of punctuation marks are used. It means knowing what to check for so that the sentences sound right and make complete sense.

In this book we look at both the making and working of grammar in a number of different ways. You can try and find out which of the ways helps you the most.

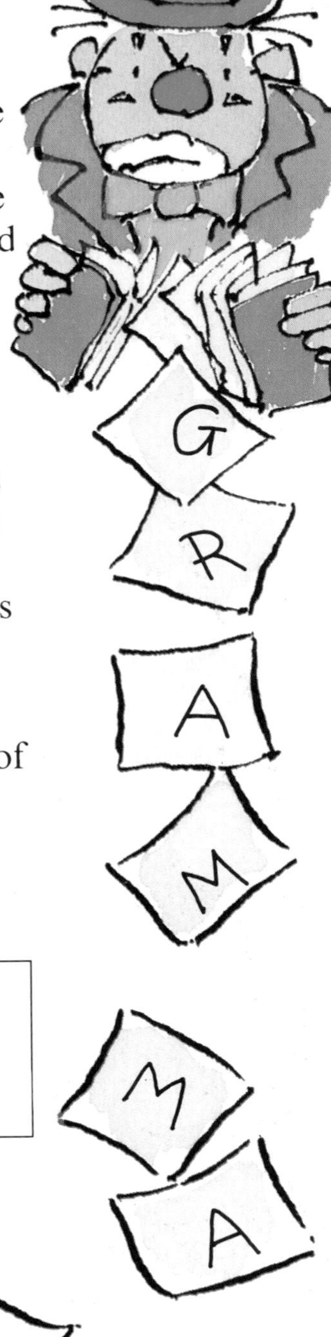

> Beware! This book is full of smart stuff. A little good grammar goes a long way. Once you have gained the skill it will stay with you for ever.

The making of grammar

Talking sense

From the moment we begin to talk we are learning grammar. We don't just copy somebody else's sentences like a parrot, we find ourselves inventing new ways of putting words together. What is more, most of what we say makes good sense or shows that we are learning fast.

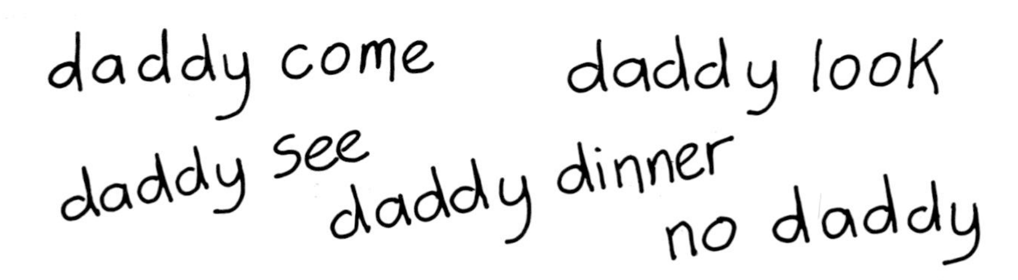

daddy come
daddy look
daddy see
daddy dinner
no daddy

In this way we start by making our own little sentences. As we want to say more and more so also do our sentences grow. Many of these first sentences are not quite like adult sentences or what we consider to be 'correct grammar', but they show an amazing natural skill for sentence-making and for making sense.

Just as we all want to talk, we also find ourselves all wanting to learn grammar, without realizing what we are doing. We do it because we want to make sense of our surroundings and to feel close to the people around us.

So, speaking clearly is the first and the most important way of learning grammar. Skilled talkers, such as lawyers, politicians and teachers have an especially good grounding in grammar.

Speak clearly

> Is talking good for us or just a waste of time? What do you think? Chat about this with a friend.

Writing just right

Setting out to write is the second most obvious way of learning the skills of grammar.

Good writing and good grammar go hand in hand. Just as understanding grammar helps us with our writing, so also does trying to write help us to know about grammar. Nobody starts learning rules before they begin writing; if we had to do that we would never ever begin. We first try writing because we want to. There are many good reasons for doing this:

We like imitating grown-ups
We like sending messages
We like labelling
We like making up stories
We like making someone else laugh, feel happy, frightened or sad
We like being authors

Having a good reason for writing helps us to write clearly and to use good grammar. In the chapter on Good Writing starting on page 95 you can learn more about the many different reasons for writing.

It is funny to think that at the same time as we are *learning to write* we are also *writing to learn* grammar and many other things. So, keep on writing; it will keep on teaching you.

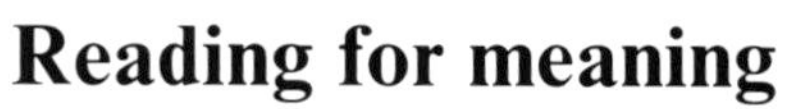

Reading for meaning

With our own talking and writing we try out and learn grammar skills for the first time. When we start reading we begin to *see* what these skills are all about.

The Iron Man came to the top of the cliff.

How far had he walked? Nobody knows. Where had he come from? Nobody knows. How was he made? Nobody knows.

Taller than a house, the Iron Man stood at the top of the cliff, on the very brink, in the darkness.

The wind sang through his iron fingers. His great iron head, shaped like a dustbin but as big as a bedroom, slowly turned to the right, slowly turned to the left. His iron ears turned, this way, that way. He was hearing the sea. His eyes, like headlamps, glowed white, then red, then infra-red, searching the sea. Never before had the Iron Man seen the sea.

He swayed in the strong wind that pressed against his back. He swayed forward, on the brink of the high cliff.

And his right foot, his enormous iron right foot, lifted – up, out, into space, and the Iron Man stepped forward, off the cliff, into nothingness.

CRRRAAAASSSSSSH!

(Reprinted by permission of Faber and Faber, Ltd. from *The Iron Man* by Ted Hughes)

The author of these words, Ted Hughes, has used grammar skills to write this story so that it is easy and

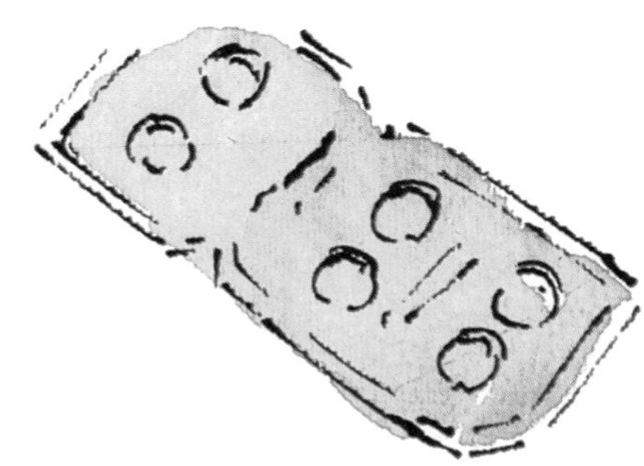

exciting to read. Supposing he had not bothered to do this:

the iron man came to the top of the cliff how far had he walked nobody knows where had he come from nobody knows how was he made nobody knows taller than . . .

If we didn't already know the story, this would be very hard to follow and to understand. But Ted Hughes arranges his words into sentences. In fact, he makes many kinds of sentences. Some of them report action. Some of them ask questions. Some of them give answers. Some of them add unusual descriptions. Some of them exclaim.

The sentences are also grouped together into several sections or paragraphs. All together, the words are skilfully arranged so that they draw you into the story and then make you want to know what is going to happen next. What is more, the spaces and other marks on the paper fit with the pauses that we find we make as we tell the story.

We are drawn into stories like this because of the good grammar. This grammar is used so well that most of the time we don't realize the trouble that has been taken in using it. By reading good examples like this we are also giving ourselves good grammar lessons.

The working of grammar

Looking at the working of grammar is rather like looking at how a complicated machine works. It works only because it is fitted together in exactly the right way. In this part of the book we are going to look at how the basic machinery of English grammar is made up and how it can best be kept in good working order.

Sentence breaking

Looking at sentences and breaking them up into parts is a good way of beginning to see how they work.

The first and easiest way of breaking sentences is to look for:

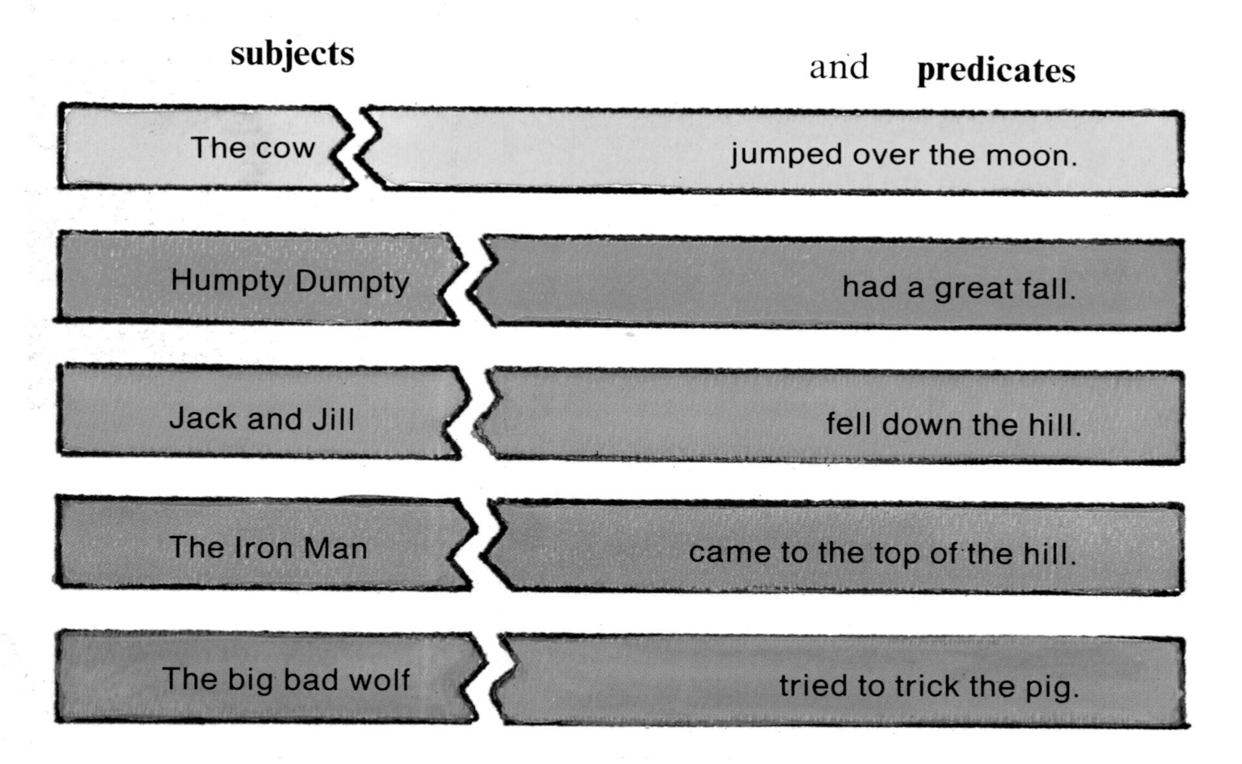

subjects
and
predicates
The cow
jumped over the moon.
Humpty Dumpty
had a great fall.
Jack and Jill
fell down the hill.
The Iron Man
came to the top of the hill.
The big bad wolf
tried to trick the pig.

The **subject** is who or what the sentence is first about. It is often at the beginning of a sentence, but not always. The **predicate** is what is said or written about the subject.

Now try and break up these sentences into subjects and predicates. (Underline the subjects.)

The sun was shining. The sky was blue. Everybody was out enjoying themselves on this lovely day. Then all of a sudden disaster struck. The ice-cream van blew up in a cloud of smoke and was never seen again.
(Answers on page 128)

We can already see that the predicate can be quite long and that it too can be broken into different parts.

A slightly more complicated way of breaking down many sentences is to look for:

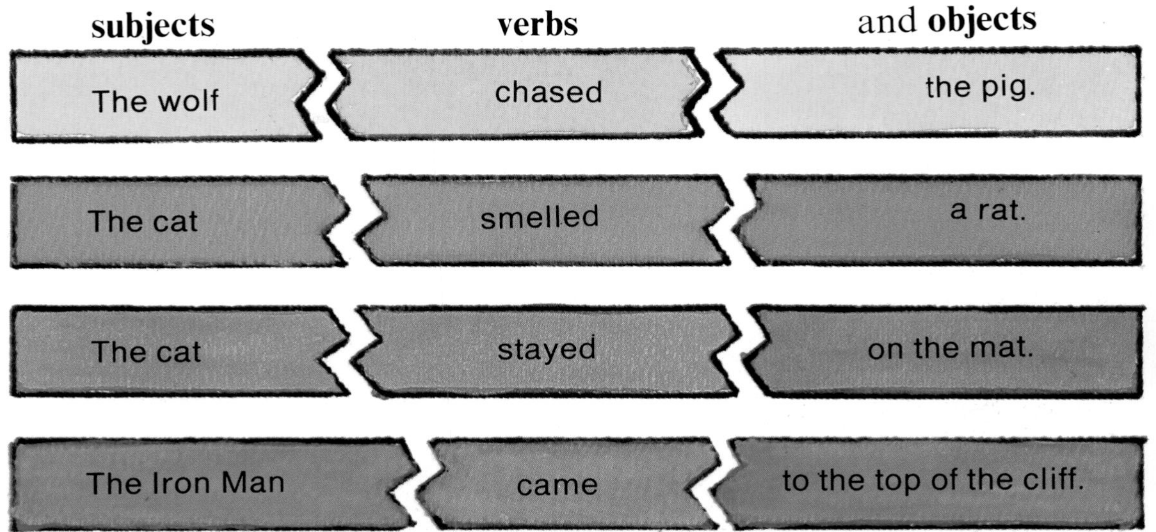

subjects
verbs
and **objects**
The wolf
chased
the pig.
The cat
smelled
a rat.
The cat
stayed
on the mat.
The Iron Man
came
to the top of the cliff.

In the first two sentences the object is simple: we say they are direct objects.

In the last two sentences the objects need extra words (prepositions): so we call them indirect objects. As we shall see (*page 84*) these can also be referred to as adverbial phrases.

But most sentences are more complicated than these simple examples. They can also be broken into parts, clauses, phrases and parts of speech. We shall now find out about the different ways of building, joining and extending sentences.

Sentence building

Sentence building is easy. We do it by making use of a small selection of building materials. These are what are generally known as *parts of speech*. Here they are:

verbs, nouns, adjectives, adverbs, prepositions, pronouns, articles, conjunctions and interjections.

Every word that we know belongs to at least one of these parts. There are also many words, as we shall see, which can belong to more than just one part.

To make it a little easier to deal with these building materials in this section we shall give them abbreviated labels:

V. N. Adj. Adv. Prep. Pro. Art. Conj. Int.

The parts of speech are also introduced and described in the Kingfisher Guide to **Good Words**.

Single word sentences

Interjections (Int.)

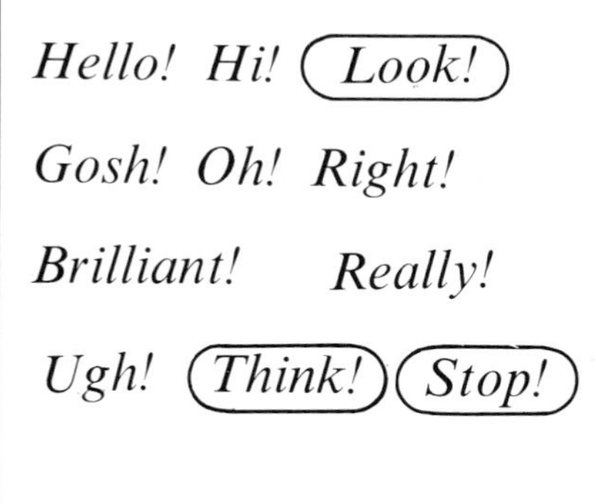

Interjections are special because they can be sentences all on their own.

Each of the particular interjections ringed above, happens also to be a verb. They are verbs used as commands (known also as *imperatives*).

See!
See how many one word orders you can make to your friend!

Two word sentences

By adding adverbs we can turn commands or exclamations into two word sentences.

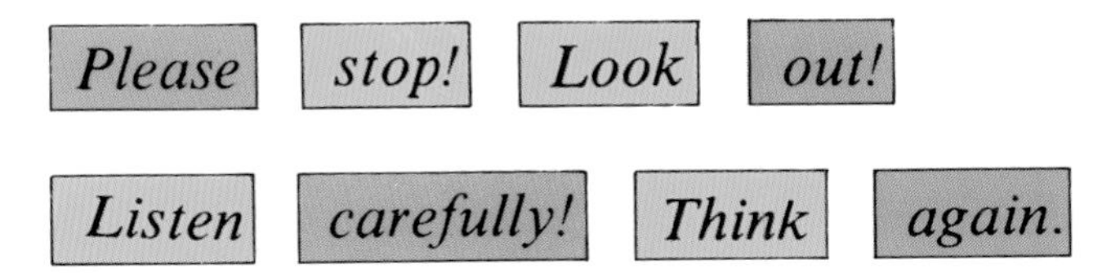

By adding certain pronouns to the verb parts we can make other two part sentences which take note of the commands.

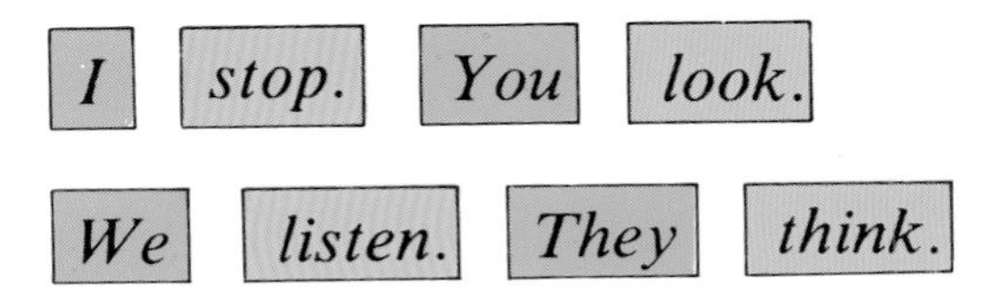

As we try to make two word sentences we quickly find ourselves wanting to use extra words or wanting to adapt words.

John stops immediately. He looks everywhere. We listen carefully to him. He and his friend think again.

> **The Key Part**
> In all these very short sentences one particular building part always appears. Can you see what it is?
>
> It's the verb – the part that shows what is happening in every sentence.

Building simple sentences

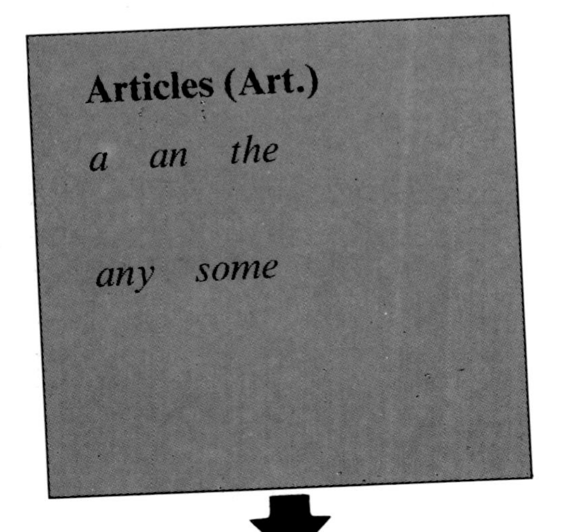

Defining or introducing words – used to point out 'which'.

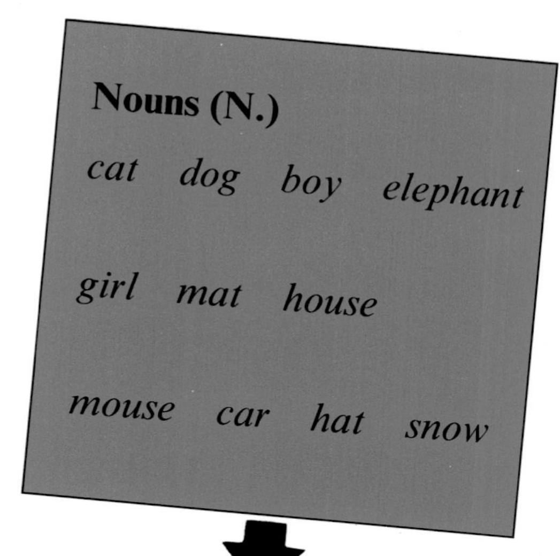

Nouns (N.)
cat dog boy elephant
girl mat house
mouse car hat snow

Naming words – words that tell who or what the sentence is about.

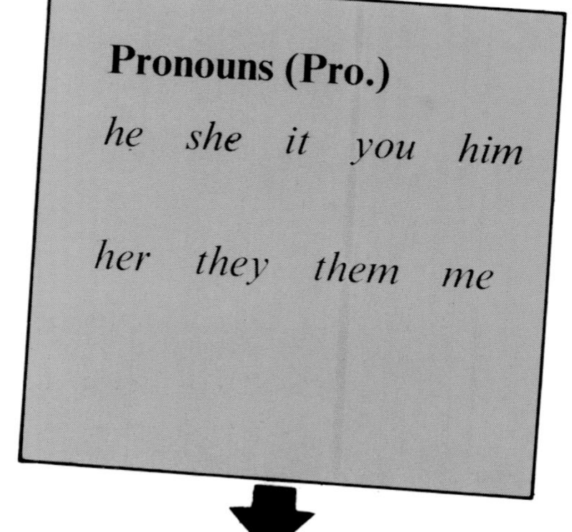

Pronouns (Pro.)
he she it you him
her they them me

Words that can take the place of nouns.

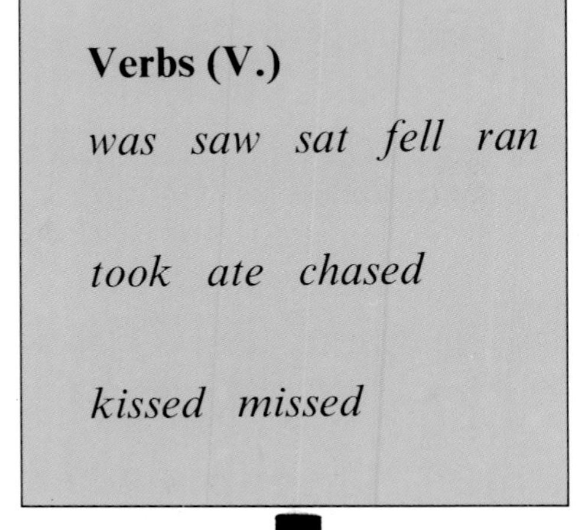

Verbs (V.)
was saw sat fell ran
took ate chased
kissed missed

The key parts to every sentence: 'doing' or 'being' words.

More Nouns (N.)

Proper nouns:
Scotland *January*

Wednesday

John *Ann* *London*

Plural nouns:
animals *children* *people*

houses *mice*

Prepositions (Prep.)

to *in* *on* *at* *with* *by*

over *before* *up*

of *under* *for* *like*

Words that introduce others, often to indicate position or, maybe, likeness.

See how many sentences you can make using the words belonging to these parts! Can you also name the parts (in abbreviation) under each word.

She	*saw*	*a*	*dragon*		
Pro.	**V.**	**Art.**	**N.**		

The	*cat*	*fell*	*under*	*the*	*elephant*
Art.	**N.**	**V.**	**Prep.**	**Art.**	**N.**

Do you find that you keep making the same kinds of sentences with the same arrangements of parts? Can you make other sentences which keep to these patterns?

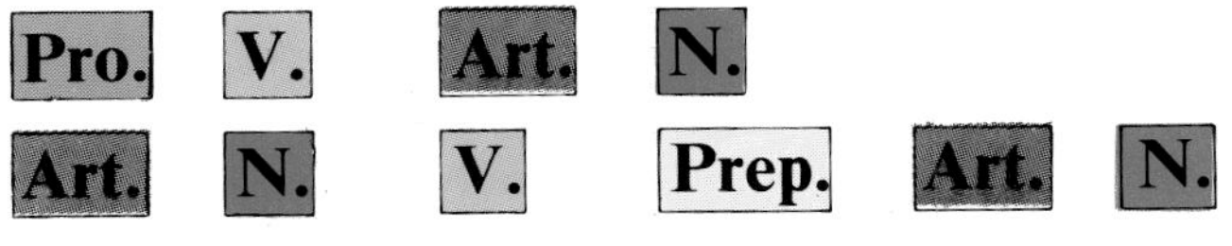

Adding adjectives

wonderful rich mysterious little huge
young old wise dirty beautiful grand
tiny blue steep high green seven six
two tumbled-down thatched red broken
smart odd pretty wintry dark moonlit
horrible surprising delightful fantastic
terrifying interesting long happy

Adjectives tell us more about nouns and sometimes pronouns.

Which of these adjectives would you fit into this story. Perhaps you could even think of some others that might fit in.

Once upon a time there lived a ______ man. He lived in a ______ house on the top of a ______ hill. The house had ______ windows a ______ roof and a ______ door. It was an extremely ______ house.

One ______ night, the ______, ______ man heard a ______ noise. He couldn't think what it was. He got out of his ______ bed. He crept downstairs and opened the door to see the most ______, ______ sight that he had ever seen. He couldn't believe his eyes.

"This is ______", he said. "This is the most ______ thing that has happened to me in the whole of my ______ life.

If we use more than one adjective with a single noun we use a comma between each one.

Other kinds of adjectives

Interrogative adjectives: *Which* book . . . ?
Demonstrative adjectives: *This* book, *that* book, *these* books and *those* books.
Possessive adjectives: *my your his her their.*

The cat . . . *This* cat . . . *My* cat . . .

(Can you see how possessive adjectives and demonstrative adjectives can take the place of articles? We can say that articles are really a weak kind of adjective)

Adding adverbs

slowly carefully
generally particularly
very quite fast
intently thoughtfully
suspiciously just
faintly gently suddenly
again always never
bitterly not

Adverbs are words which are often added into sentences next to verbs. We use them to say *more* about a verb. We can also use them to tell us more about adjectives (*very* good or *disgustingly* bad) and other adverbs (*very badly* or *extremely well*).

Which of these adverbs would fit into this story?

The cat got up ______ from the mat. She looked ______ around the room. She listened ______ ______ for any suspicious noises. She sniffed the air ______ for any suspicious smells. She crept ______ to the corner of the room. She thought she could ______ smell a rat. ______ she sprang over the television and pounced. Miaow! Out she came with a ______ smelly, old shoe in her mouth. She was ______ disappointed. She was determined ______ to be fooled ______.

Adapting Verbs

Verbs can play amazing tricks. Any verb can be adapted into many different forms to make a sentence completely change its meaning.

As well as saying 'The acrobat balances skilfully on a tightrope', we could say 'She balanced',

'She is balancing'

'She was balancing'

'She has balanced'

'She will balance'

'She will have balanced'

'She would have balanced'

'She may balance'

'She would balance'

'She could balance'

'She may have balanced'

'She could have balanced'

'She should have balanced'

'She should balance'

The balancing depends on all kinds of times and conditions – or what we call the different tenses of the verb *balance*. Most of these different tenses depend on using extra verbs – auxiliary verbs. Each of them gives a distinctly different meaning to the sentences. If we add the negative adverb *not* another whole set of meanings arise just as happens if we turn them into questions (She could not balance. Does she balance? etc.).

Jumping through hoops

The lion jumps through the hoop.

Can you adapt the verb *jump* to show its many different aspects?

Making verbs agree

Verbs are also good at changing themselves to suit their subjects. For instance, when we are writing we say:

I sit	you sit	he sits	we sit	they sit
I am	you are	he is	we are	they are
I have	you have	he has	we have	they have
I was	you were	he was	we were	they were

The dog *eats* biscuits.

Dogs *eat* biscuits.

The cat *bites*.

Some cats *bite*.

We know how to make verbs agree by having a good eye and ear for language we see and hear around us.

Playing about with parts

The great thing to remember about fitting parts of speech together is that many words can act in more than one part. They can be like circus performers who can do a variety of tricks.

For instance, a good few words can double up as nouns and adjectives.

A Fight (N.)

We can say that *pink* (N.) is a pretty colour but also that the umbrella is *pink* (Adj.).
We can talk about *umbrellas* (N.) or about an *umbrella* (Adj.) shape.

A good few words can double up as verbs and nouns.

We can have a *fight* (N.) or we can *fight* (V.).
We can say that he went *fishing* (V.) and that the *fishing* (N.) was a success.

They are Fighting (V.)

Some words can also act as both adverbs and adjectives, or as both prepositions and adverbs.

The car went *fast* (Adv.) because it was a *fast* (Adj.) car. It sped *away* (Adv.); *away over* (Prep.) the hill it sped.

We also have many special tricks for changing parts, especially by adding suffixes (. . . ness, . . . ful, . . . ly, etc.) as we see in the Guide to **Good Words**.

> So you see! Simple sentence building is easy. All we have to do is to choose the right parts, adapt them and change them around, if necessary, and then place them together to make sense.

Sentence joining

Conjunctions

and or but yet

Conjunctions are words which join other words together or sentences together.

Can you decide which conjunction is best for each joining space?

The elephants led the parade ______ were followed by the horses. All the animals performed beautifully ______ the clowns behaved very badly. They threw water at the audience ______ covered themselves in custard pies. We could not decide whether we liked the acrobats best ______ whether we preferred the jugglers.

If we only speak or write in short simple sentences our language quickly becomes jerky and uncomfortable. So we often use conjunctions to join up sentences.

Conjunctions in pairs

either . . . or *neither . . . nor*

not only . . . but also

both . . . and

Subordinating conjunctions

like before when

if because . . .

Words which introduce extra clauses into sentences. We shall look at these in the next section.

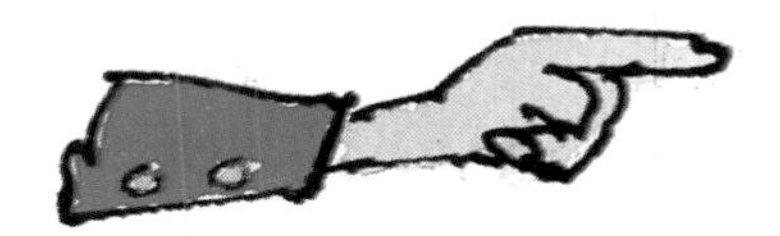

Sentence extending

The clown fell over.

The clown with the funny face fell

The clown whose face was brightly painted fell into the

Extending sentences means making them longer and more interesting. Instead of thinking just of individual words we can begin to think of different groups within a sentence. These groups can also act like single parts of speech. We call these extensions phrases and clauses.

Phrases

A phrase is a group of words which does not make complete sense on its own. It has no verb.

Adjectival phrases act as extended adjectives, adding descriptions.

The cat *with the white spot* caught a rat.
The girl *sitting at the back* was talking.

Adverbial phrases act as extended adverbs, answering the questions How? When? Why? and Where? about the verb.

The cat caught the rat *in the barn.*
The girl was talking *all the time.*

Noun phrases act as nouns.

Both the cat and the girl were friends.
A phrase is *a group of words without a verb.*

into a bucket of water.
water because he was tripped up.

Clauses

A clause is a group of words with a verb. Sentences often contain more than one clause, a main clause and a subordinate clause or two.

She began talking	*when she was one.*
He ate two pies	*because he was so hungry.*
These are main clauses	These are subordinate or secondary clauses

The subordinate clauses in this case also happen to be adverbial clauses, adding to the verb in the main clause.

Adjectival clauses often begin with *who, which, that, whose* or *whom.*

The boy *who was always eating pies* was very fat.
The girl *whom I saw in the road* was an amazing sight.

Noun clauses act as nouns.

I saw *what she was doing.*
We knew *that he was eating.*

Build your own extensions!
See how many different ways you can extend these simple sentences with phrases and clauses: *The mouse climbed onto the giant. The princess met a frog.*

Sentence punctuating

Punctuating means making points. It means putting the right kind of points in just the right place so as to point out the length, shape and exact meaning of sentences.

[.] [?] [!] **Full stops**, **question marks** and **exclamation marks** all point out sentence endings.

Full stops are at the end of sentences that are statements. Question marks indicate questions. Don't they?

Look out! Please use !!! for orders and exclamations!

These are the most important markers for every sentence.

Stops also have extra uses.
If part of a sentence is missing . . .
A short row of stops also has its uses, as you see.
Also, a single stop can be used for shortening some titles or names. *Sun. 14th Feb. J. Smith*

[,] **Commas** point out brief pauses in a sentence.

● They can help, for instance, to distinguish the different sections of extended longer sentences, which we talked about on the previous page.

● They are useful when we make lists of words, or have a list of succeeding main clauses.

There were elephants, lions, kangaroos and penguins. The elephants stood still, the lions growled, the kangaroos hopped away and the penguins just flapped around.

> Notice how we don't usually put a comma before the conjunction *and*!

[“] [”] **“Inverted commas** are used to show words that are directly spoken”, said the teacher. She added, “They are also called speech marks because they are put at both the beginning and the end of the words actually spoken”.

['s] **Apostrophes** by the letter *s* indicate belonging.

John's bike *Jane's speedboat*

We have to be careful when the belonger word also ends in *s* like *boys*: we then say *the boys' bikes*.

Apostrophes are also used to show missing letters in shortened words or shortened combined words:

3 o'clock (of the) don't can't they're we'll (we will or shall)

[:] **Colons** can be used before a list of items like this: jam; sugar; cheese; biscuits; bread and butter.
[;] We can use **semi-colons** to separate each item or we could also use commas in this case. Semi-colons can also be used as a stronger natural break in a longer sentence; otherwise we might use a conjunction.

[-] **Hyphens** are used to join two words which are linked together like *seat-belts jelly-babies* and so on. A set of two hyphens - indicating an extra comment - can also be used in the middle of sentences in the same way as brackets ( ) are used.

Underlining a word gives it special emphasis.

She was sitting on his hat. (but not anymore)

She was sitting on his hat. (not anyone else's)

She was sitting on his hat. (not his gloves)

Sentence style

Style is the personal touch which makes sentences look and sound appealing. The working of grammar needs style every bit as much as it needs the correct fitting together of parts, phrases and clauses.

Here are a few tips about style:

Vary the length of sentences.
To make sentences follow each other comfortably it helps to make them of different lengths. Some may be short. Others may be longer with clauses and sub clauses which make them more complicated.

Vary the building patterns of sentences.
Try and start the sentences in different ways.

Avoid repetition of important words or phrases.
Using pronouns instead of nouns can often help. It is also helpful to find synonyms (different words with similar meanings such as *difficult* and *hard*).

Remember who you are writing for.
Try to keep their interest.

Use words which sound good together.
Enjoy the thrills and skills of good grammar!
Strive for style!
This is what poets do especially. It is always good to have an ear for the sound patterns of words as well as an eye for the way words look together.

Remember, lastly, who you are or the sort of person you wish your readers to think you are.
It's your personal style which shapes your writing.

Sentence translation

Learning another language can teach us a lot about the working of our own grammar.

Many of the ways we use to look at English grammar come from the study of Latin, the language of the Ancient Romans. Latin grammar follows its own rules, using fewer words than English.

LATIN
Feles nigra in stoream sedebat

cat black on mat was sitting

ENGLISH
The black cat was sitting on the mat.

FRENCH
Le chat noir s' était assis sur le tapis.

The cat black itself was seated on the mat.

In French it takes 9 words to say the same thing, as opposed to 5 in Latin and 8 in English.

URDU

پر بیٹھی ہے کالی بلی قالین

mat cat black Is sat on

In Urdu the sentence is made up from right to left with 6 words.

Each of these four languages (English, Latin, French and Urdu) uses different numbers of words, different kinds of words and different word arrangements in order to make the same meaning. They each have their own special grammars.

So you see, grammars are keys for unlocking languages. That is why they are so useful.

Sentence checking

All good writers like to check their sentences after they have finished their writing. They want to be sure that the grammar is working well. It often helps to have the help of another reader such as a friend, a teacher or editor – someone who is a trained expert at such work. Here are some of the questions writers and editors ask themselves when checking sentences:

1 Do all the sentences begin and end correctly?

Make sure the first word of each sentence has a capital letter and that the sentence ends with a full-stop, a question mark or an exclamation mark.

G ~~g~~ood grammar needs careful attention.

2 Do all the sentences have a verb?

Verbs [are] absolutely essential for all proper sentences.

3 Are the sentences too long?

Look out for sentences that go on and on, leaving you breathless and confused! As a general rule it is advisable not to use more than one single conjunction (*and or but*) in any sentence.

The boy ran down the road. ~~and~~ [H]~~h~~e went round the corner and ~~then~~ he saw an elephant. ~~and~~ [H]~~h~~e went for a ride and all his friends waved.

4 Are nouns and pronouns used wisely?

Good writers try to avoid repeating the same nouns because [they] ~~good writers~~ know how useful pronouns can be. They also know that [Pronouns] ~~they~~ should only be used when who or what is being referred to is unmistakable.

Re-read and check

Are there any other possible double meanings?

5

Be careful about the placing of extra phrases or clauses!

The fire was put out before any damage was done by the fire brigade.

Are all the natural pauses (and asides) correctly punctuated?

6

Remember, punctuation pays off. Doesn't it?

Do the verbs keep to the same tense?

7

Stories can be told in a present tense or in a past tense. It does not make sense to change tense.

The clowns enter. They fall over each other. They throw custard pies and they ~~ran~~ run away.

Are there any 'split infinitives'?

8

'Infinitives' are verbs in their basic form with the word *to* in front of them like *to be, to put* or *to read.*

It is easy to carelessly put adverbs in the middle of infinitives. Split infinitives are usually rather clumsy to comfortably read.

Is the writing up to *Standard*?

9

Avoid using slang or language which is generally not understood or accepted by everybody. We expect writing to be more polished than the language of ordinary talking. This is what we call *Standard English.*

10

Does each sentence really make sense?

Sentence Sense

Welcome to the circus!
Learn the skills!
Enjoy the thrills!
It all makes sense
with sentences.

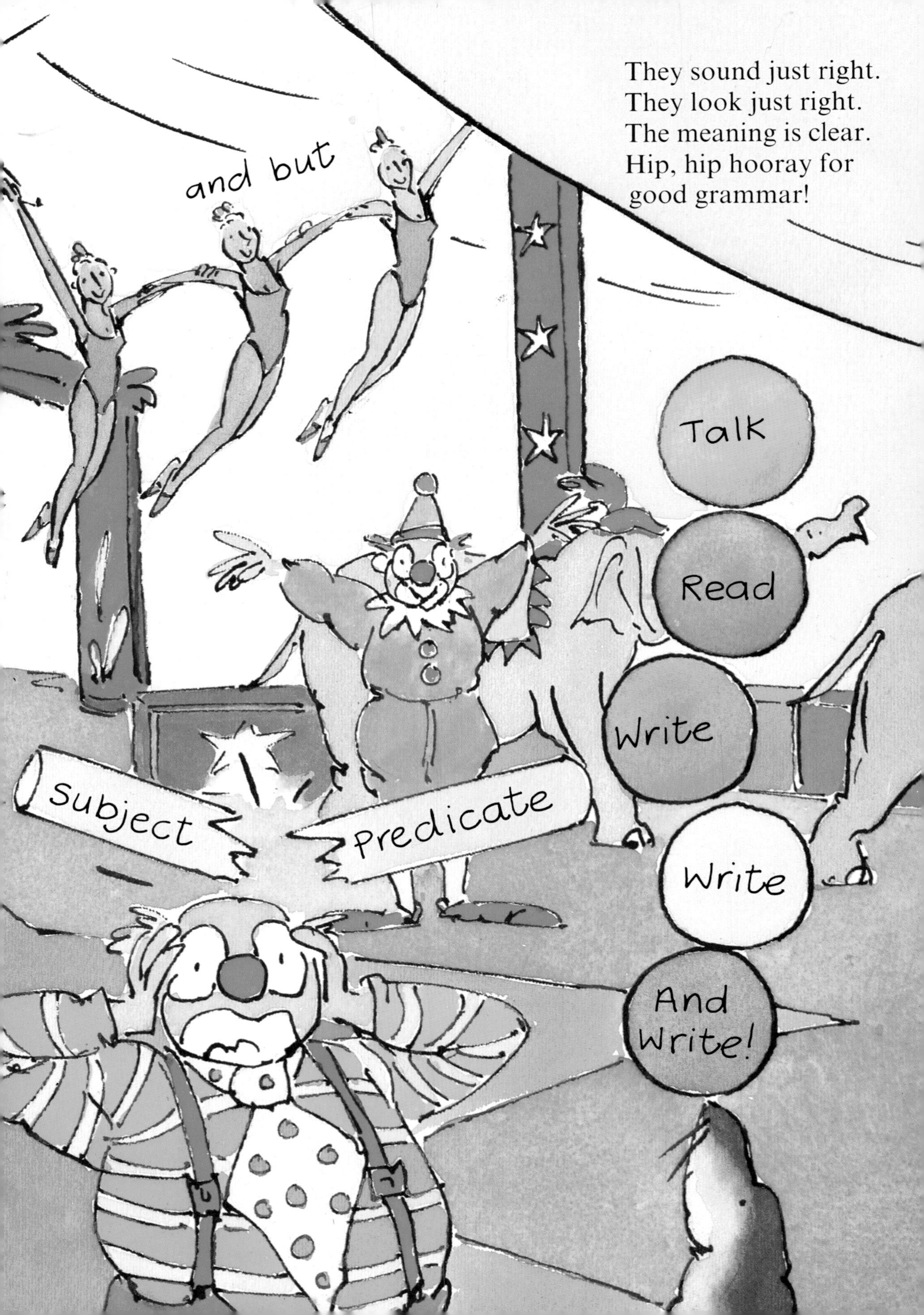
They sound just right.
They look just right.
The meaning is clear.
Hip, hip hooray for
good grammar!
and but
Talk
Read
Write
Write
And
Write!
subject
Predicate

GOOD WRITING

The Guide

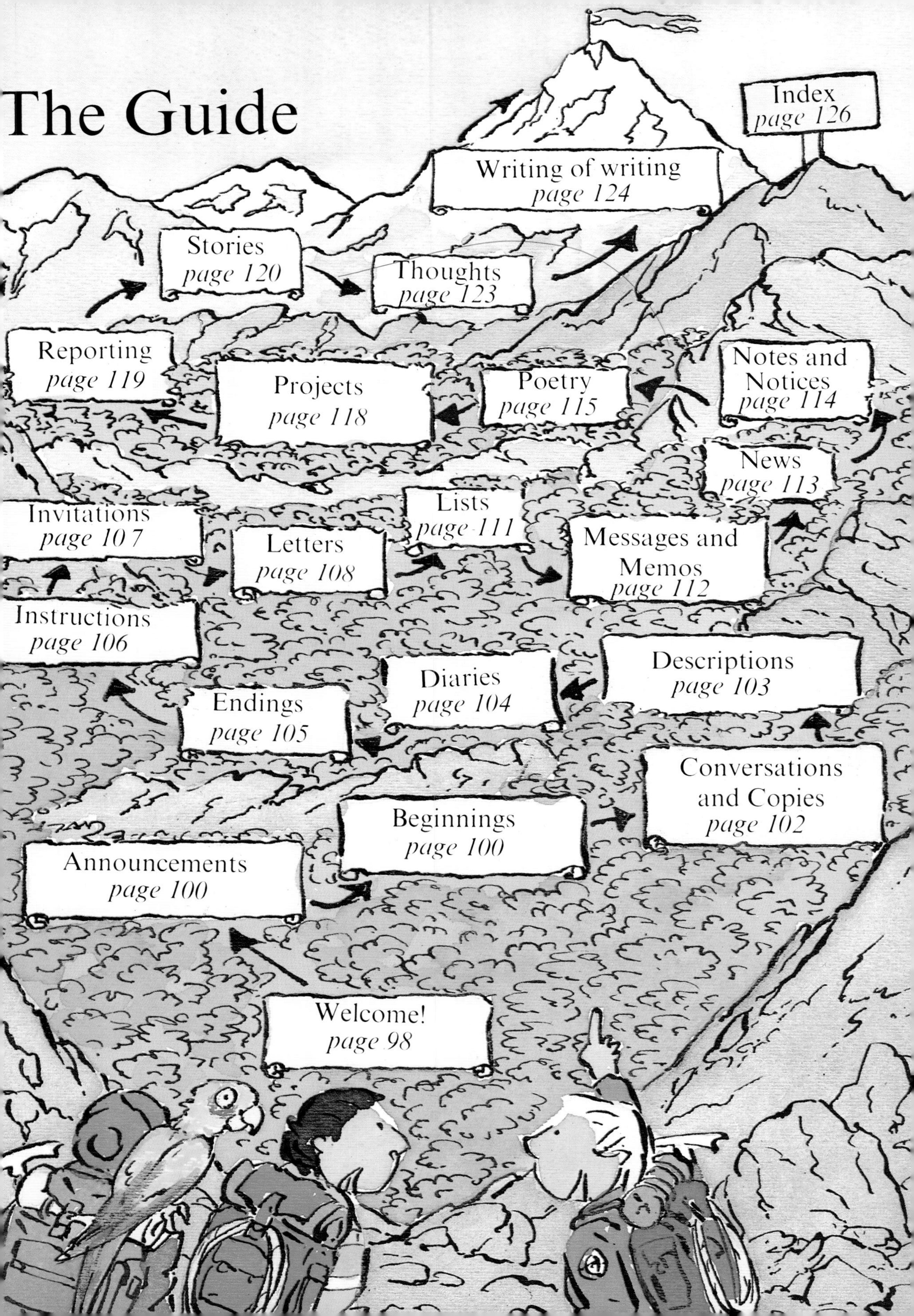

Index
page 126
Writing of writing
page 124
Stories
page 120
Thoughts
page 123
Reporting
page 119
Projects
page 118
Poetry
page 115
Notes and Notices
page 114
News
page 113
Lists
page 111
Invitations
page 107
Letters
page 108
Messages and Memos
page 112
Instructions
page 106
Descriptions
page 103
Diaries
page 104
Endings
page 105
Conversations and Copies
page 102
Beginnings
page 100
Announcements
page 100
Welcome!
page 98

Welcome!

Welcome to the world of writing!

Good writing is just like exploring. Good writers need courage, good ears, good eyes and good minds. Then, if they have something to write with and something to write on, the world is theirs. There are so many paths to take with so many people, places and times to meet.

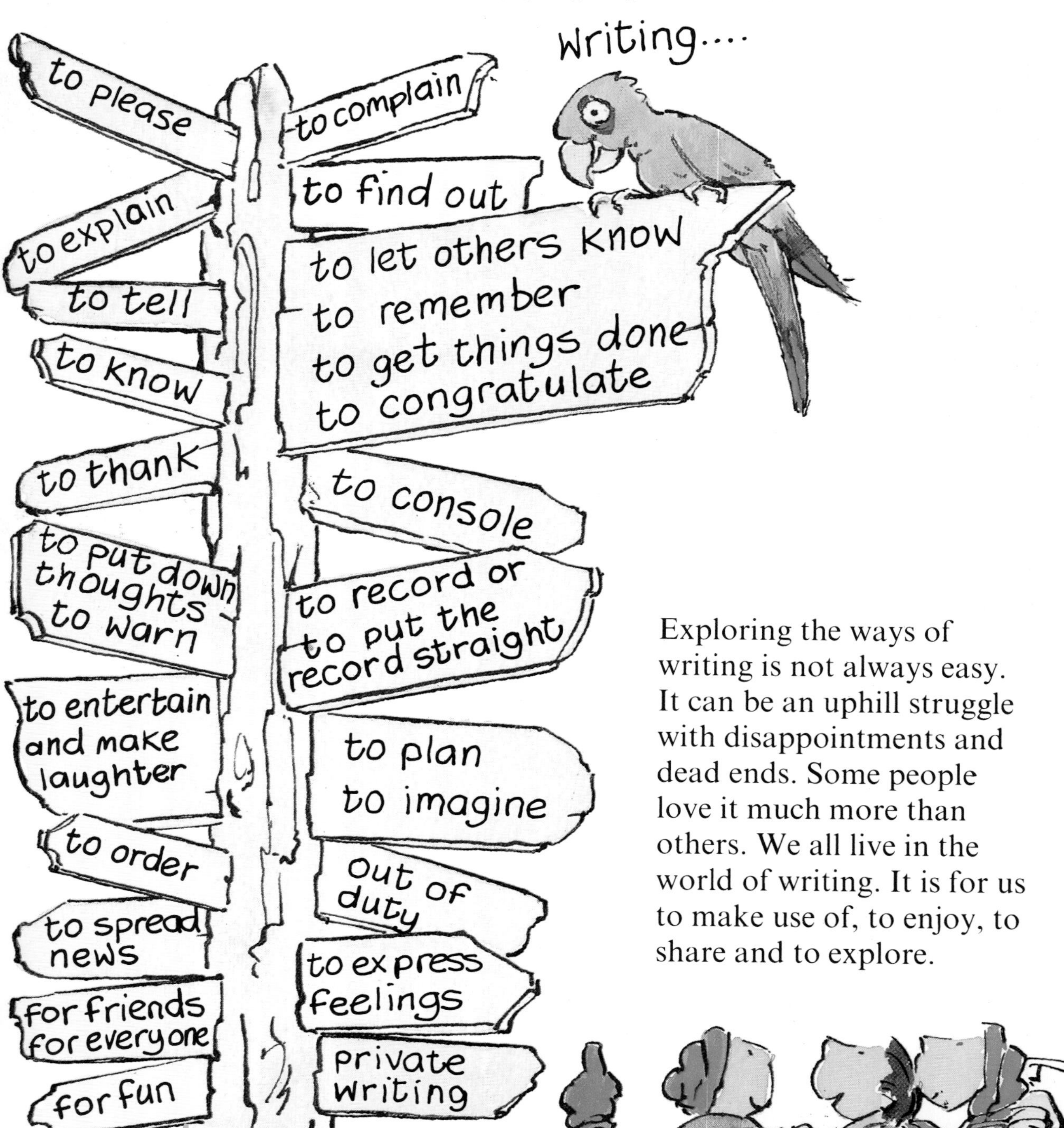

Exploring the ways of writing is not always easy. It can be an uphill struggle with disappointments and dead ends. Some people love it much more than others. We all live in the world of writing. It is for us to make use of, to enjoy, to share and to explore.

Exciting times for writing

These are now exciting times for writing. There are so many gadgets and machines to help us write, from all kinds of pencils and pens to typewriters, computers, copiers and so on. There are also machines that save us from writing such as telephones, recording machines, cameras, televisions and so on. Will writing die out and someday be taken over by new inventions altogether?

But not to worry! The world is more full of writing than ever before. Each year the numbers of books, papers and amounts of writing multiply. More and more people are writing and we seem to be writing even more and more. Writing is certainly here to stay for a good while.

Writing to save time

Can this be so? Surely it is easier and quicker to say words than to write them. Yes it is, but spoken words usually disappear for ever. If you write them down the words are saved for as long as you like. And anyway most of us can read them much faster than we can speak them. Not only can writing save ideas and news, it can also play with them, imagine them or plan them. Writing saves all kinds of time.

Talking Time
This book now takes us on a grand exploration of many of the ways of writing. Good writing can be catching. It will easily spread and go to your head. But it always takes time. So Take Care and Good Luck!

Announcements

Congratulations to all readers of this book.
You have embarked on an exciting mission.

Passengers are advised that the next voyage to the unknown will start at midnight

Mr and Mrs Brer Rabbit would like to announce the birth of four sweet bunnies.

These are short easy ways of making information, intentions or feelings known. We all have special announcements to make at times. Try putting one on the door of your room and see if anybody takes notice.

Beginnings

How shall we begin? Oh dear! I don't know what to write first. I'm afraid of spoiling the nice clean page. Oh! Panic stations! Let's have a cup of coffee instead.

coffee for beginners

Many writers say they feel like this before they start working. Beginnings can be the hardest part of writing.

Here are a few ways of helping to get started:

- Try a practice start. Put down all your first ideas quickly without worrying about the order, spelling, handwriting, etc. Then play around with them and use the best bits for a real start. But don't forget you can always change it again later.

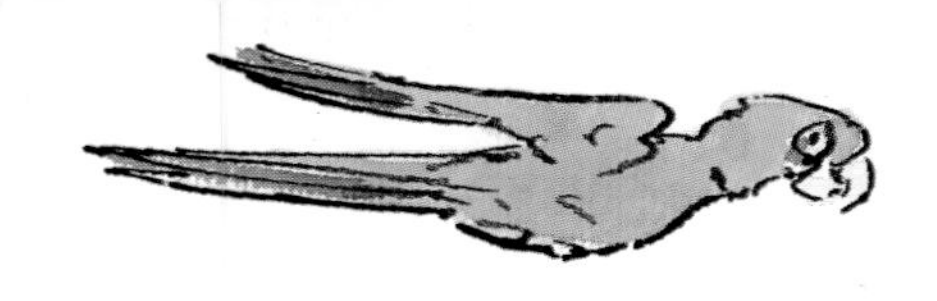

● Start with a bold simple title:

PARROTS

● Follow with a general statement on what you are writing about.

Parrots can be very puzzling.

● Use a traditional opening.

Once upon a time ...
There was once ...

● Set the scene (give an idea of the time and place of what you are writing about).

When I was on my way to school last Friday ...

● Start dramatically:

'Bang!' – the door slammed and Sally was left alone with a bucket stuck to her right foot, clutching the frightened pink rabbit.

● Begin with a few words that create a special atmosphere of expectation:

It was a dark and stormy night ...
Deep, deep in the forest ...
Where is the green parrot?
The Iron Man came to the top of the hill ...

● Remember that the first words are really like an advertisement for all the writing that is to follow. They have to be enticing.

> You have no excuses now – pick up your pen and write!

Copies

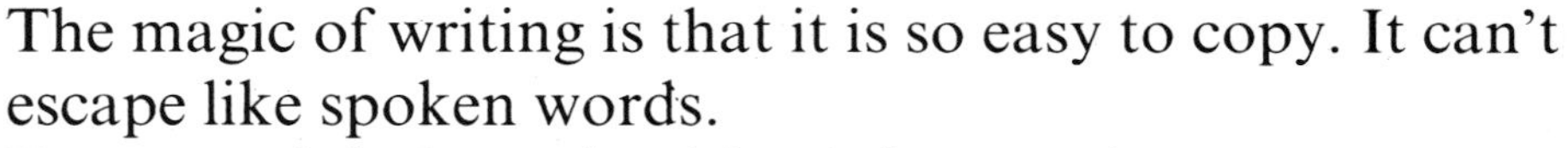

The magic of writing is that it is so easy to copy. It can't escape like spoken words.
For a special piece of writing it is sometimes necessary to make two or three different copies before you can get it just as you want it. Good writers are never afraid to keep on making changes.

The Intrepid Explorers

The three explorers set off on a mission to reach the top of the world. They took a large map and some secret instructions and a hefty supply of baked beans.

The Intrepid Explorers
On Friday the first of June the three explorers set off from Brighton on a mission to reach the top of the world. They took a large map, some secret instructions, and a hefty supply of baked beans.

Once you have done all your changes then you can use a printer or a photo-copier to make as many samples of the final draft as you like.

Conversations

"Mum, I don't want to go to school," said Tom.
"You know you have to go," replied his mother.
"But the children dislike me and so do the teachers," moaned Tom.
"Tom don't be so silly, you have to go, you're the Headmaster," said his mother.

We have special ways of showing speech in writing. We use a type of punctuation called speech marks ("" or '') which we put at the beginning and the end of the actual words that are being spoken. We also always start a new line each time somebody new is speaking.

Descriptions

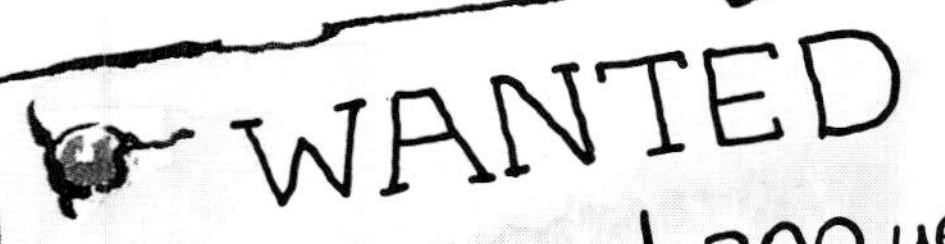
WANTED
Female – aged 200 years.
3metres tall with a pink
and green hairstyle. Last
seen in the middle of the
North sea wearing
orange trousers and a
shiny green jumper.
WARNING – Do not
approach this woman –
but contact your local
Police Station

Descriptions are like pictures. They are ways of using words to give an idea of what a person, place or event is like. Sometimes we need good descriptions so that we can identify somebody or something we are looking for.

Descriptions can be used to make writing more interesting.
We can say

The door closed.

or we give more detail and say

The old red wooden door swung on its rusty hinges and closed with an ominous creak.

Can you add descriptions to make these sentences more interesting?

Jane went down the road.
The dog barked.

What's this?
An enormous four-footed animal. It has a very, very long nose which it uses like a hand to pick up things . It has big floppy ears and is usually grey.

Answer – An elephant

Try giving a description of an animal or an object to your friend, without using your hands. Can they guess what you mean?

Diaries

Writing a diary is usually a personal matter. It's a way of recording events and personal thoughts. It can be like having a conversation with yourself.

Monday 6th February Mum says if I don't tidy up my bedroom she is going to stop my pocket money for five weeks.

Tuesday 7th February Dad has sided with mum. At this rate I won't get any pocket money for another 3 years.

Wednesday 8th February I decided I might as well give in and tidy. By bedtime I had only got as far as crawling under my bed. I found an apple core, 3 odd socks, my best catapult, an old shoe and two years of my favourite comics.

Thursday 9th February Dad says it's all going into the bin if I don't do something before the Friday deadline. I moved around a few boxes but it didn't convince mum.

Friday 10th February Things are getting really bad – I think I might have to run away Even my teacher says I'm untidy – he made me stay in at playtime and clean my desk. I told him that brilliant people are always untidy but I don't think he believed me.

Saturday 11th February Gave in and tidied up (just hope they don't look in my wardrobe) – now it doesn't even look like my room. When I'm grown up I'll remember this. If I ever have any children I'll allow them to be brilliant and untidy.

Sunday 12th February Too exhausted from tiding up to do or write anything.

It's fun keeping your own diary. Try writing one in a notebook. Enjoy using it – but only when you have got something to say – otherwise it might become a chore. Think of a diary as a secret friend – but remember to keep it in a safe place!

Endings

Endings are important as they are the last words and thoughts that a reader is left with.

"They came to the river, they came to the bridge – they crossed it hand in hand – then over the hills and far away she danced with Pigling Bland!"

(From *The Tale of Pigling Bland* by Beatrix Potter, © Frederick Warne & Co., 1913, 1987.)

Endings can be neatly finished off –

... and so they all lived happily ever after.

– or they can leave us to decide our own conclusions, allowing us to complete the story as we want to. This is called an open ending.

and so they came to the top of the hill. They looked about them and wondered where they would go next.

THE END

Instructions

Instructions tell you how to make or do something. Often there are diagrams to help, that go with the writing. It is usually a good idea to list the instructions in careful order.

TO MAKE A PAPER DART

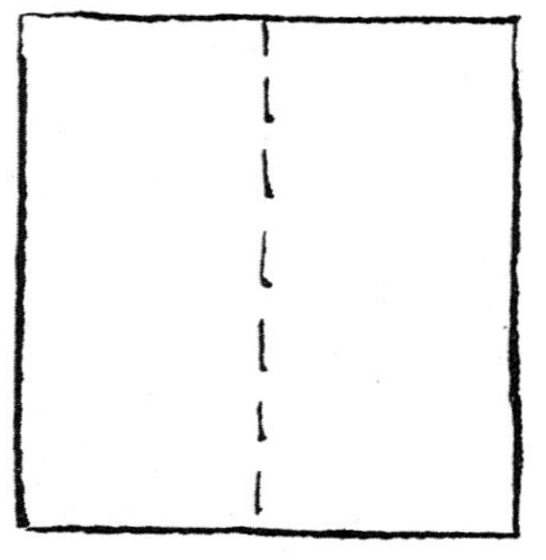

1 Take a rectangular piece of paper and fold it in half in line with the longer side. Then unfold it again so that you can see the crease.

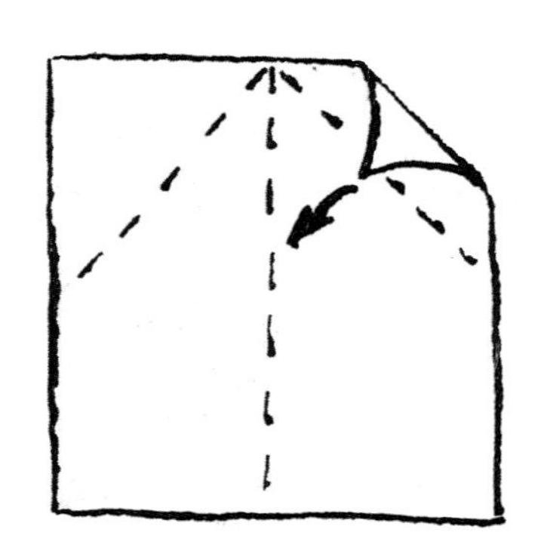

2 Now fold the top two corners to meet the middle crease.

. . . .

Can you complete these instructions so that you are finished with a good design? Or perhaps you could write instructions on how to make one of your favourite meals, a bed, a surprise or even a mess?

HOW TO CROSS THE QUICK SANDS
Strap boards onto feet
Follow the red arrows
Never stop still!

Instructions always need to be followed carefully stage by stage. It is very easy to get them wrong. So it is best to make them as simple and as straightforward as possible.

Invitations

Invitations ask you to attend an event. It is best to make them look bright, colourful and inviting.

COME TO A PARTY
Julie invites you to her birthday party on 3rd June
5pm ~ 9pm
R.S.V.P

R.S.V.P. stands for *Répondez s'il vous plaît* the French for *reply if you please*.

> So how about having a party and making some invitations?

Jokes

There was a parrot who liked writing
Especially about something exciting
He flew into the air
And hijacked a bear
Now isn't that something worth writing?

Often we think that writing has to be a serious business and that it is always hard work. Give up that idea. *Righting* is far more fun than fighting. It's almost as delightful as writing (GROAN!).

Letters

There are many different reasons for writing letters.
Some we do out of duty:

29 December

24 Royal Road
Crabtree
Yorkshire
TLN 4EP

Dear Uncle Fred,

Thank you very much for giving me your old school tie for Christmas. The colours of orange, yellow and red will go very well with my new green shirt and dad says it will prove very useful.

I hope you had a good Christmas with aunt May and uncle Joe. By the way, did you give Cousin Rosie an old school tie as well?

Hope you are fit and well. Once again thank you,

Your loving nephew,

Ben

I can't ever imagine receiving a worse present-mean old so and so!
What revolting colours but I'd better humour the old chap.

Sometimes we have to write letters like this because it is the polite thing to do. We have to try and please the person we are writing to. It is best to try and make it fun rather than a chore. There is a set way of presenting your letter with, for example, the address on your right (as shown above).

There are non-personal letters that you need to write for more formal reasons, such as to do with business.

In this case it is important to lay out the beginning and end of your letter in the customary way, including adding the name and address of the company or department you are writing to:

24 Royal Road,
Crabtree,
Yorkshire
TLN 4EP

Fun Travel Ltd.,
22 Back Street,
Bristol
BR 2GA

23rd February 1990

Dear Sir or Madam,

I have read about your special fun holidays in the African Jungle. I enclose a stamped addressed envelope and would be pleased if you could send me a free brochure with details of cheap fares for sensible children.

Yours faithfully,

Ann Jones

Ms Ann Jones

When we are writing formal letters to people we don't know at all it is usual to end with *Yours faithfully* or *Yours truly*. If we know who the person is then it is best to use his or her name (Dear Ms Smith) and conclude with *Yours sincerely*.

Try looking through the magazines and see if there is anything interesting to send away for, or even complain about. Set out your letter like the one here.

There are also friendly letters that we really enjoy writing and receiving – chatty letters to friends, for instance.

My Place
Sat night

Dear Clare,

Hello - sorry it's so long since I've written but I have been very busy My cat has had kittens - they are so cute - the smallest one is ginger and white and so naughty! I hope your mum and dad let you come to stay and then you can come and see them.

Last week I got my photos back from the holiday - there are some really good ones of you in the pool. I'm putting one in the envelope for you.

I hope school is okay - we are doing a really boring topic at the moment - on butterflies again - would you believe it!

Write back soon

Love Sue
xxx

fan letters

Letters to friends are often like a written telephone conversation (and usually much cheaper) and do not have to be 'correct' English. They can be very chatty and lots of fun to read and write. So next time you have a chance, pen a few lines to a friend, or even to your old granny on her own. Enjoy it!

love letters

enquiry letters

complaining letters

congratulations letters

apology letters

Lists

Friends and phone numbers
Sally 343434
Sunita 29642
Mick and Shirley 185634
Jin Hee 123456
Angela 654321

Shopping
sugar
eggs
biscuits
jam
honey
bread
milk
coffee

Menu
Soup 50p
Sausage, beans and chips £1.20
Fish and chips £1.40
Hamburger 90p
Cheeseburger £1
Hot Dog 60p
Tea 25p
Coffee 30p

Reminders
Feed the cat
Hang out the washing
Fetch the paper
Phone Fred
Prepare tea

What I want for Xmas
New bike
Football kit
A computer
sweets

Favourite footballers or popstars

____

____

____

____

____

Spellings
knee
key
knife
comb
bomb
gnome
tongue
sign

Messages and Memos

IMPORTANT!!
Must remember to collect the cat from the vet at 5pm

I'm stranded on a desert Island

These are the kinds of messages that we usually write on scraps of paper to remind ourselves or to tell our friends simple bits of information, requests or maybe endearments. They are really little letters passed around in an informal way.

People who work in offices are always sending messages to each other and they usually call these memos (memoranda). They have a correct way of doing them to make sure there is no misunderstanding.

MEMO

TO Jane Smith DATE 3rd June

FROM Sally White TIME 4 pm

MESSAGE Could you find out all the details from the Wilson's file?

News

Latest News

EXPLORERS IN NARROW ESCAPE

Three explorers and a parrot yesterday narrowly escaped being buried in an avalanche. They had just successfully crossed the dangerous quicksands to reach the mountains when they heard an almighty rumbling from above. Not a moment too soon . . .
(continued on page 3)

Teachers tighten rules

Anybody found running in the corridors will in future be punished severely. The headmaster went blue in the face as he said "This is the very last warning . . ."

Ringmer School Football Team win Tournament

On Saturday our team won 5 out of the 6 matches to become the district champions. Our player of the tournament was Neil who saved the day with his brilliant goalkeeping.

Newspapers and news-sheets are an excellent way of making use of good writing. We all like to read the latest news. Journalists, the people who write newspapers, have particular ways of writing which easily catch attention. Snappy headlines are a good idea as well as short sharp sentences.

Computers (especially with desktop publishing programs) and photocopiers make the production of newspapers quite easy.

The fastest known speed is the speed of light. Light travels at 299,792.5 kilometres per second. Scientists have discovered that light always travels through space at exactly that speed. It never goes faster or slower.

Notes

Notes are usually a shortened form of writing. A short letter or message is sometimes called a note. But we also talk of making notes when we mean making a shortened form of something which is said or written.

Note-making or note-taking is a useful skill that allows us to keep a brief written record of anything we want.

When somebody is speaking, it is impossible to write down every word but we can just write a few words to indicate the main points that are being made.

light has fastest speed – 299,792.5 km per sec, never changes

We usually write such notes just for ourselves so they don't have to be in correct English as long as they make sense to us.

Notes can also be made from a piece of writing that we want to shorten or we want to remind ourselves of.

NB (Please Note) Good note-making pays off.

Notices

NETBALL TEAM FOR SATURDAY

C J. Wright GK K. Long
WA P. Lemon GD P. Cass
WD F Sharp
GA L. Pine

IMPORTANT – Meet at 9am at School

Notices are a way of spreading information. They are usually put up in an obvious place such as a noticeboard. Have you any notices on your wall?

Poetry

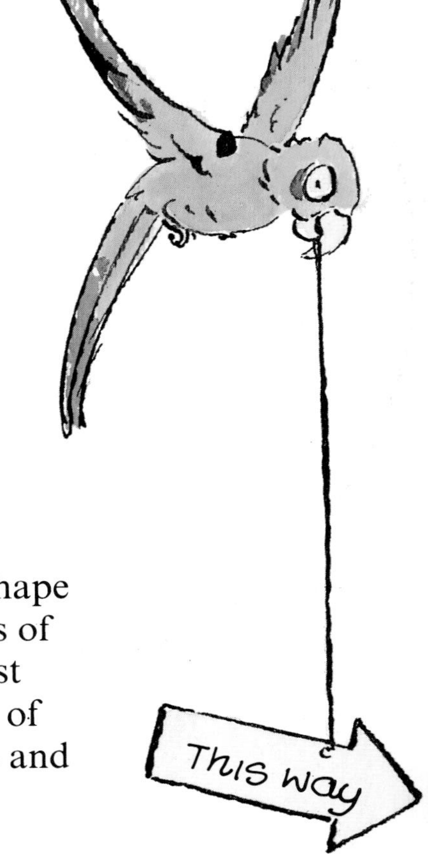

Poetry is poetry
It may be good
It may be bad
It may be happy
It may be sad.

Some like poetry
Some detest it
Some write it beautifully
By now you must have guessed it.

(Peter, aged 9, from *Young Writers Young Readers*,
reprinted by permission of Boris Ford, the editor.)

Poems are like people – they can come in any size, shape or form. Writing poetry is different from other kinds of writing because it allows us to play with words in just the way we like. We can even bend the normal ways of grammar, change spellings or even make new words and sounds.

Gust Becos I Cud Not Spel

Gust becos I cud not Spel
It did not mean I was daft
When the boys in school red my riting
Some of them laffed.

("Gargling with Jelly" by Brian Patten
from *Gargling with Jelly*, © Brian Patten, 1985.
Published by Viking Kestrel and in Puffin Books.)

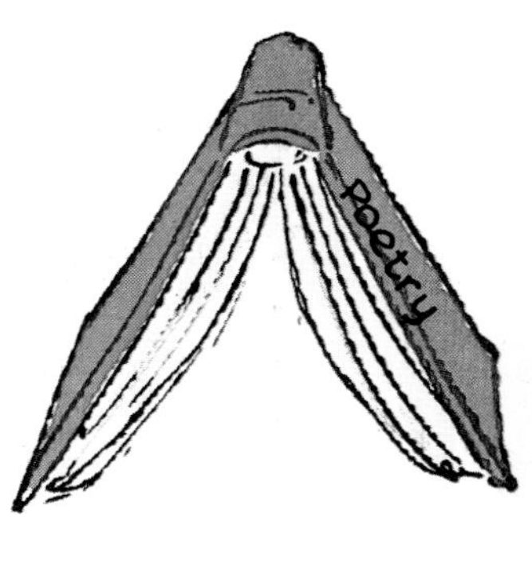

The great thing about poems is that you can control them just how you like. They can never be wrong. What is more, a poem can be your thoughts on paper about anything you choose.

Mum and dad feeling mad,
Little me feeling sad.

Just take the words and line by line,
Think of things you want to say,
Then rearrange and play and play.
Until at last it sounds just right,
Then read it aloud or hide it out of sight.

It is important to remember that poems do not have to rhyme. They can also pay attention to the sound patterns in other ways. For instance poetry can follow a strict and regular rhythmic pattern.

Breathless
(written at 21,200 feet on May 23rd)

Heart aches,
Lungs pant,
The dry air
Sorry, scant.
Legs lift
And why at all?
Loose drift,
Heavy fall.
Prod the snow
Its easiest way;
A flat step,
Is holiday.

(From "Breathless" by Wilfrid Noyce;
reprinted by permission of Wm. Heinemann, Ltd.)

This poem can give us the feeling of the steady rhythm of climbing the mountain. The short lines help show the breathlessness.

lorries - tigers
roaring / hot breath
fumes - jungle of
colours - people /
insects scurry-
ing – houses /
trees / towering

You can write poems about places you have visited, things you have seen, things that have happened to you, and those created by your imagination. Anytime you think of a few words you like jot them down in a notebook and you can use some of them in a poem later.

The tiger lorries roared passed
The hot fume breath misted the air.
Out of control they raced down the hill,
Dodging in and out,
Miraculously missing the scurrying people
Reds, greens, purples, oranges, yellows,
Gay and gaudy amongst the brick grey
  and concrete jungle.
The chattering motorbikes-screaming,
To a halt at the traffic lights
Animal like obeying the jungle law.

You can draft (rewrite) your poem as many times as you like, until you get one poem or several poems that you are happy with.

So, poetry is poetry – you can make it do what you like. Try it and see for yourself. You can never go wrong.

Projects

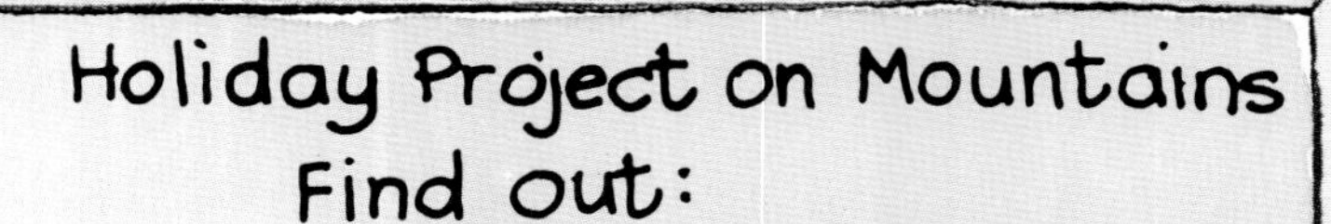

Holiday Project on Mountains
Find out:
How they were formed
When they were built
Which is the highest
Mountains under the sea
Mountain wildlife
Mountain climbers
What are volcanoes

Doing a project in school usually involves finding out and collecting information about a particular subject, be it dinosaurs, explorers or parrots. The basic meaning of the noun *project* is actually *a plan*. Doing a good project therefore depends on making good plans. One way to start is to make a list of questions about what you might want to find out:

Where do parrots come from?
What are the best-known parrots?
Where do they naturally make their nests?
Is it cruel to keep them as pets?
How are they tamed? etc . . . .

Information books and encyclopedias will help you get started, but accounts of any first-hand experience that you or any of your friends may have will make it much more interesting. Projects are also good opportunities for making models and pictures, but it is your own writing which will bring them all together.

Reporting

Putting it down in writing: this is what we do when we want words to really stick. There are many occasions when we do this.

School Report

Name: *Edward Lock* Class: *2W*

Subject	Gradé	Comment
English	*B*	*He is lively in oral work but lacks concentration in writing*
Mathematics	*C*	*Could do better.*

REPORT OF NATURE CLUB

On Friday 24th April the nature club went for a ramble through the woods. They saw carpets of bluebells, two squirrels playing on an oak tree and a stray parrot. Everybody wondered where the parrot had come from.

Agreement

I promise to pay Thomas £2 for cleaning my car

Signed *Date*

Swimming Certificate

This is to certify that

Susan Lock

has swum 200 metres breaststroke.

Date: Signed

26.7.89 *D Gardner*

Once any kind of written record is made it can be seen or examined by anyone and at any time. This kind of writing needs to be done with care. To help us there are often set ways of doing them. The best reports are fair and not too long. As we shall see next, a report about something that has happened can also be a good story.

Stories

Everyday stories

"Do you know what happened last night! I had just finished my tea and was looking out of the window when I saw this strange thing moving along the garden fence. I went outside and saw this amazing bird . . . ."

Stories all the time

They go on anywhere and everywhere. Everything that happens makes a story – it only needs someone to tell it. In fact, most of us are bursting with stories all the time just from our everyday lives:

What happened?

Last night? On Saturday morning? Just now? During the holidays? At breakfast? Under the bed? At the end of the garden? At your gran's? To the cat? When you were much younger? On that day you will never forget? And whenever and wherever you have been?

Every story is special

Stories grow from gossip. Sometimes the same story gets better and better with each telling. Sometimes, too, we can make them really good by taking the trouble to write them down. We then have to choose the bits of the story that matter most to us. Each story-teller or writer has her or his own way of doing this. That's what makes stories fun to read. We know that each one is going to be different.

Is there a special way of writing everyday stories? Not really. It is probably best first to write the story just as it comes to you. You may find that you get carried away with it. Let that happen and then afterwards look at it as a reader and you may want to trim it or check the sentences. Then polish the beginning and ending.

Imagined Stories

As everybody knows, *telling stories* does not necessarily mean telling the truth. If you get fed up with trying to tell ordinary stories, it can be fun, for a change, to tell a story made from the most deliberate lies that you can think of.

> Bobby pulled at the bucket on his foot but it was well and truly stuck. The telephone rang, he leapt up, slid on the floor and fell on the cream trifle. Just at that moment his Mum got home from work.
> "I can explain, honestly," stuttered Bobby.

But most made-up stories have some truth in them, usually to do with feelings, such as of sadness, fear, worry, excitement, joy, or whatever. If you try writing about a lonely pig you will find yourself writing about what you know personally about loneliness. Good fairy-tales do just this kind of thing and that is why they are so popular and so satisfying to write.

> See what truths you discover if you write about *The Sad Banana, The Silly Sausage, The Greedy Grasshopper, The Angry Ant, The Unhappy Elephant, The Lazy Lollipop, The Ugly Duckling* or about things or creatures of a special nature.

Horrors, especially, can make spellbinding stories.

> Amelia sat up in bed quickly. Something had woken her, she knew it wasn't normal. The rain tried to get in her window, the wind moaned her name and Amelia clutched her teddy tightly and waited . . .

Stories in any shape or size

Round stories

They were arguing over the last jar of honey. It was so boring... Andy fell asleep. He dreamed that he was sailing across the sea in a pea-green boat with the owl and the pussy-cat

Tall stories

Did I ever tell
you about the time
I saw a pig fly?
Well, it was one
of those funny days
in summer when
everywhere is hazy
with heat. I was
having an argument
with some friends
when one said "the
day that's true then
pigs will fly". Just
at that moment I saw
a pig fly past the
window. It seemed
strange but they
never believed me.

Short slippery stories

The
snake
slithered
silently
through
the
grass
until
at
last
it
reached
the
pond.
Then
it
slipped
gracefully
into
the water never to be seen
again.

Longer stories

To write longer stories it is often best to plan them with chapters:

Chapter One	The Explorers set off
Chapter Two	Danger in the Forest
Chapter Three	Parrot to the Rescue
Chapter Four	In and out of the Quicksand

Thoughts

Spare a thought.

We are always having thoughts all the time. Unless we write them down, they are usually lost forever. Of course, it would be impossible and pointless to keep a record of all our thoughts. All the same, writing can be a useful way of helping us to sort out ideas and pin down our more valuable thoughts.

Idle thoughts
Most of us have times when we find ourselves just thinking or day-dreaming. What are your thoughts when you're lying in bed?

Special thoughts
What are your thoughts about good friends, bedtime, fairies or ghosts?

Remember that it is your own thoughts that make you and your writing special. Hold them carefully. They will take you far.

Writing of writing

Well done all of you who have followed our ways of writing! You have reached the top of the world. You can write of anything for anyone. You can even write of writing.

Writing can be tough
Writing can be fun
Writing can . . . .

And don't forget the magic of spelling,
the treasure of words
and the skills and thrills of grammar.
They won't forget you. They will follow you and assist you wherever you write.

writing
words
Writers are right. All good writers know that there is always more to explore. They know especially that there is always so much to learn from each other. So keep on travelling – Good wishes to everybody while you *WRITE*, *WRITE* and *WRITE*.

Index

Answers to pages 24 and 25

2 Too wise you are
Too wise you be
I see you are
Too wise for me

3 (a) camel
(b) bees
(c) leopard
(d) pig
(e) lion & otter

4 Palindromes
These are words or groups of words which read the same backwards as they do forwards.

5 (a) Ireland
(b) Iran
(c) Argentina
(d) Poland
(e) Finland
(f) Canada

1 T	O	2 M	■	3 C	■	4 G	E	5 M
O	■	A	■	R	■	N	■	E
■	6 O	C	T	O	P	U	7 S	■
■	A	■	■	S	■	■	I	■
8 C	R	O	S	S	W	9 O	R	10 D
O	■	■	■	W	■	L	■	R
11 C	R	12 O	C	O	D	I	L	E
O	■	U	■	R	■	V	■	A
13 A	I	R	■	D	■	14 E	L	M

Answers to page 73
The subjects are "The sun", "The sky", "Everybody", "disaster" and "The ice-cream van". All the other words make up the predicates.